CHÁVEZ

CHÁVEZ

A Distinctive American Clan of New Mexico

Facsimile of 1989 Edition

by
Fray Angélico Chávez

New Foreword
by
Marc Simmons

SANTA FE

Sunstone books may be purchased for educational, business, or sales promotional use. For information please write: Special Markets Department, Sunstone Press, P.O. Box 2321, Santa Fe, New Mexico 87504-2321.

printed on acid free paper

Library of Congress Cataloging-in-Publication Data

Chavez, Angelico, 1910-1996.
Chávez : a distinctive American clan of New Mexico / by Fray Angelico Chávez ; new foreword by Marc Simmons.
p. cm. -- (Southwest heritage series)
"Facsimile of 1989 edition."
Originally published: Santa Fe, N.M. : W. Gannon, 1989.
ISBN 978-0-86534-653-6 (softcover : alk. paper)
1. Chavez family. 2. New Mexico--Genealogy. I. Title.
CS71.C499 2009
929'.10720789--dc22
2009003931

WWW.SUNSTONEPRESS.COM
SUNSTONE PRESS / POST OFFICE BOX 2321 / SANTA FE, NM 87504-2321 /USA
(505) 988-4418 / ORDERS ONLY (800) 243-5644 / FAX (505) 988-1025

The Southwest Heritage Series is dedicated to Jody Ellis and Marcia Muth Miller, the founders of Sunstone Press, whose original purpose and vision continues to inspire and motivate our publications.

CONTENTS

SOUTHWEST HERITAGE SERIES

I

THE SOUTHWEST HERITAGE SERIES

"The past is not dead. In fact, it's not even past."
—William Faulkner, *Requiem for a Nun*

The history of the United States is written in hundreds of regional histories and literary works. Those letters, essays, memoirs, biographies and even collections of fiction are often first-hand accounts by people who wanted to memorialize an event, a person or simply record for posterity the concerns and issues of the times. Many of these accounts have been lost, destroyed or overlooked. Some are in private or public collections but deemed to be in too fragile condition to permit handling by contemporary readers and researchers.

However, now with the application of twenty-first century technology, nineteenth and twentieth century material can be reprinted and made accessible to the general public. These early writings are the DNA of our history and culture and are essential to understanding the present in terms of the past.

The Southwest Heritage Series is a form of literary preservation. Heritage by definition implies legacy and these early works are our legacy from those who have gone before us. To properly present and preserve that legacy, no changes in style or contents have been made. The material reprinted stands on its own as it first appeared. The point of view is that of the author and the era in which he or she lived. We would not expect photographs of people from the past to be re-imaged with modern clothes, hair styles and backgrounds. We should not, therefore, expect their ideas and personal philosophies to reflect our modern concepts.

Remember, reading their words and sharing their thoughts is a passport back into understanding how the past was shaped and how it influenced today's world.

Our hope is that new access to these older books will provide readers with a challenging and exciting experience.

II

FOREWORD TO THIS EDITION
by
Marc Simmons

He has been called a renaissance man and New Mexico's foremost twentieth-century humanist by biographer Ellen McCracken. Any way you measure his career, Fray Angélico Chávez was an unexpected phenomenon in the wide and sunlit land of the American Southwest.

His life, which began at Wagon Mound, New Mexico in 1910, was filled with vigorous physical and intellectual activity. Above all, Fray Angélico was an independent and original thinker, traits not usually associated with someone in a religious order who takes a vow of humility.

In the decades following his ordination as a Franciscan priest in 1937, Chávez performed the difficult duties of an isolated backcountry pastor. His assignments included Hispanic villages and Indian pueblos. As an army chaplain in World War II, he accompanied troops in bloody landings on Pacific islands, claiming afterwards that because of his small stature, Japanese bullets always missed him.

In time despite heavy clerical duties, Fray Angélico managed to become an author of note, as well as something of an artist and muralist. Upon all of his endeavors, one finds, understandably, the imprint of his religious perspective. During nearly seventy years of writing, he published almost two dozen books. Among them were novels, essays, poetry, biographies, and histories. Sunstone Press is now bringing back into print some of the rare titles.

Upon his death in 1996, Chávez left his huge collection of documents and personal papers to Santa Fe's Palace of the Governor's History Library, one of the region's major research institutions. In that year, it was renamed the Fray Angélico Chávez Library and Photographic Archives.

Today, a handsome life-size statue of the *padre* in his Franciscan robe stands in front of the building on Washington Avenue. During the first severe winter after its unveiling, a good Samaritan placed a stocking cap on the head of the statue.

Throughout his life, Fray Angélico remained a confirmed Hispanophile. In the 1960s and 1970s, that stance won him the enmity of Chicano Activists, who rejected the Spanish side of their heritage. But Fray Angélico had spent too many years documenting the colonial record of New Mexicans' achievements on this far-flung frontier to succumb to the blandishments of anti-Spanish ideologues.

Indeed, of the many accolades he received in his lifetime, none pleased him more than the one bestowed upon him by Spain's King Juan Carlos: membership in the knightly Order of Isabel la Católica, granted in recognition of his contributions to learning and the arts.

All true aficionado's of the American Southwest's history and culture will profit by collecting and reading the significant body of work left to us by the remarkable Fray Angélico Chávez.

III

FACSIMILE OF 1989 EDITION

CHÁVEZ

A Distinctive American Clan
Of New Mexico

Books by Fray Angelico Chavez

POETRY

Clothed with the Sun

The Single Rose

Eleven Lady-Lyrics

The Virgin of Port Lligat

Selected Poems

BELLES-LETTRES

New Mexico Triptych

From an Altar Screen

The Lady from Toledo

The Song of Francis

My Penitente Land

La Conquistadora

HISTORY

Our Lady of the Conquest
Archives of the Archdiocese of Santa Fe
Origins of New Mexico Families in the Spanish Colonial Period
Coronado's Friars, 1540-1542
New Mexico Roots, Ltd. (Ms. in U. of New Mexico Library)
Missions of New Mexico, 1776 (with Eleanor B. Adams)
The Oroz Codex, Franciscans of New Spain, 1523-1597
The Domínguez-Escalante Journal, 1776
Chávez: A Distinctive American Clan of New Mexico

BIOGRAPHY

But Time and Chance (Padre Martínez of Taos)
Très Macho: He Said (Padre Gallegos of Albuquerque)

CHÁVEZ

A Distinctive American Clan
Of New Mexico

BY FRAY ANGELICO CHAVEZ

To

ROBERT FORTUNE SANCHEZ

Tenth Archbishop of Santa Fe
Great Friend and Benefactor

Contents

Illustrations

A Most Necessary Introduction

Foreseeing highly raised eyebrows at specific words on the title, and no less the ornate crest, one makes haste to smooth them back with proper explanations. First, "*distinctive*" refers primarily to a large family's very early start in a region of our country first settled by European stock; also for its having had, if tenuously so, some sort of remote noble background. It is likewise distinctive for having had a single Name Ancestor who had come from Spain. There were many other Chaves individuals, likewise from the Extremaduran homeland of Cortés and Pizarro, who were among the first so-called Conquistadores in different parts of the New World. The prime example is one Nuflo de Chaves of Extremadura who left his full name in a province at the bottom of South America. The surname of New Mexico's much less famous progenitor, also from Extremadura, likewise survives, if much more humbly than Nuflo's, in a small town and a county.

Secondly, "*American*," over and above denoting our Western Hemisphere, emphasizes the fact that this New Mexico family, along with some others, got its start here several years before Jamestown and Plymouth Rock, besides acquiring United States citizenship decades before Ellis Island felt a flood of immigrants from every other European country. And more significantly in this regard, it is truly American for having come to acquire some Native American infusions, in varying degrees and at various periods, down the lengthy course of almost four hundred years. Finally, when it comes to national defense, New Mexico's Chaves men have come to the foré, from a Union brevet general and a couple of lieutenant colonels as early as the Civil War, down to increasingly larger numbers of patriots in every armed conflict ever since.

As for the word "*clan*," a Gaelic derivation which the Scots have rightfully made their own, it is the only one we have in English to denote groups of families harking back to a common Name Ancestor, both through the paternal and maternal lines. Moreover, the heraldic crosses of St. Andrew displayed upon the crest provide a good excuse for using the term. This will be further explained anon.

Then there is the "*Chávez*" spelling of the name on the title. It is now the almost exclusive one used in New Mexico, although it is not a patronym, having had its start relatively late toward the end of the last century. The original

"*Chaves*" comes from the Latin plural *claves* for keys—as displayed upon the crest—which in Galician Spanish (and Portuguese) had evolved into *chaves* while in Castilian Spanish it turned into *llaves*. Although the surname is not patronymic, meaning "the son of" as in Rodríguez or Martínez, the zet had already been added in Portugal long ago. It also became the common spelling in neighboring Mexico, and from there it made its way here in modern times.

Lastly, our Chaves pioneer ancestors are most distinctive, if we must put it so, for having left no sumptuous mansions filled with all sorts of accumulated memorabilia like those found in other centers of Latin America and New England, no rare works of art which included painted portraits of each generation's haughty sire, no libraries crammed with learned tomes of the times besides stacks of documents detailing inheritances and other family fortunes. All that the first pioneers left in this regard were bare adobe memories which time and the weather kept washing away. This is because their beloved land of New Mexico, so much isolated for centuries as she was from the outside world, could offer them little else than that same perishable adobe which, in many ways, is part of her charm.

Still, we are most fortunate that the land's few extant records do provide surprisingly ample material on the distinctive part which the pioneer Chaves folk played among their less-documented contemporaries. Hence this ancestral account is likewise distinctive in itself. *Unlike some other name histories published elsewhere, it tells all, at least all that we know—from humbler ethnic or social admixtures down the generations to particular incidents which society or religious circles deem shameful or far from noble. After all, nothing has changed ever since Eve made Adam bite Lilith's apple and old Abraham had a bastard brat out of Hagar.*

* * *

All of which brings us to the last term in the title, "*New Mexico*," both as a distinctive name and as an entity.

Her name goes far back to 1581-1583 when some soldiers and three Franciscan friars first came up the Rio Brave del Norte (now the Rio Grande) looking for "*la nueva Mexico*," a fabulous land rich with gold to plunder and souls to save. The soldiers returned empty-handed while the friars who remained behind were slain by the Middle Rio Grande natives, and then an expedition sent up to ascertain the friars' fate finally confirmed the name. It was a feminine designation, after the golden Aztec City of Mexico which Hernán Cortés had conquered, and also plundered, some sixty years before. Ever since then a firm belief had grown about this far northern *terra incognita*, where the rich Aztecs were said to have originated, as another such city of Mexico, a *new* Mexico, waiting to be plundered by the adventurers and saved by the missionaries.

This feminine name the Spanish Crown used when authorizing Don Juan de Oñate to colonize the land in 1598, and then in 1609 when it constituted the colony as *El Reyno de la Nueva México*, still under the false belief that its as yet unmapped surroundings, if not actually containing golden cities, offered a shorter route to the wealth of India and Cathay. *La Nueva México* was also in the title of Gaspár de Villagrá's epic poem on the Oñate Conquest, which he published back in Spain in 1610. (The name's masculinization was influenced quite early by the maps of French and Italian cartographers who used the male terms *Le Nouveau Mexique* and *Il Nuovo Messico*.) At any rate, New Mexico got her distinctive name *two hundred and forty years* before there was a Republic called Mexico south of here. Moreover, she was under Spain for almost two centuries and a quarter and only twenty-five years under newly-born Mexico; and, finally, has been an integral part of the United States for almost a century and a half.

Her long past history, however, was never as glorious as her royal name sounds. As some of the early Chaves men used to say, she was a "miserable kingdom" while under Spain, due to her long isolation from the rest of Spanish America and the entire civilized world. This was also caused by a string of evil royal governors who were sent up periodically, and who made life miserable for colonists, missionaries, and local Indians alike—what brought on that terrible Pueblo Revolt of 1680. What did bring about some improvement in the following century (1694-1800) began with the arrival of new colonists, but still there was plenty of misery, again due to the land's continuing isolation, and steadily worsened this time by the growing strength of the ferocious Indians of the surrounding plains and deserts. Some further improvement came from closer contacts, brief though these were, with the new Republic of Mexico, along with the development during this period of the Chihuahua Trail from the south and the Missouri-Santa Fe Trail from the northeast (1821-1846). But it was only a few individuals, not the people at large, who profited from this new economy.

It was not until 1846, when the United States took over, that life began to improve at a more rapid pace, and again mainly among those few individuals just mentioned. But ever since then each succeeding decade gradually brought about the cultural and material American prosperity which New Mexico, as one of the Fifty States, enjoys today.

All of what has been said so far brings up the ethnic quality of her original colonists and that of their descendants down to our times. It is a most important question, and one to be clarified for the instruction of our own Hispanic inhabitants as well as for the inquiring newcomer. The viceregal orders to Oñate specified that his 1598-1600 colonists had to be *españoles*, as were also those later ones in 1694-1695. But the term "*español*" had a particular meaning in New Spain in those times. As Salvador de Madariaga once pointed out, the first individuals from Spain were designated according to their provinces of origin, while the adjective *español* became a noun to denote any New World people who were considered to be Spanish. Many of the early Spaniards in New Spain had married Indian women, and then those *mestizo* or *coyote* children of theirs who kept intermarrying with others of pure Spanish blood (or predominantly so) were finally recognized officially as honest-to-goodness *españoles*. They were "restored" Spaniards, as it were. (The Spaniard Don Juan de Oñate himself is a most appropriate example here, since his wife was descended from the Aztec Emperor Moctezuma, and their children were well restored by now.)

And so a number of the first New Mexico colonists, those of a third generation born down in southern New Spain, were such "restored" *españoles*, and more so those who came decades later. Then, as time went by, when one or the other of their own grandchildren happened to acquire some local Indian blood by hook or crook, they were labeled *mestizos* or *coyotes*. These, provided they kept intermarrying with others having predominantly Spanish blood (and having reacquired a Caucasian look whether dark or fair), became "restored" *españoles*—a process carried on *ad infinitum* as in the rest of Spanish America. However, this type of *mestizaje* or admixture was never near as thick and widespread as the one in a vastly more populated New Spain, later Mexico, where the Indianic element greatly outnumbered the Hispanic.

This is by no means an exclusive Hispanic phenomenon. There are countless "restored whites" in other parts of our nation going back to colonial times, and not merely among the lower classes. I remember reading as a youth an article in the old Colliers magazine which told how some brash fellow from a high-society family, one closely allied to the heroes of the Civil War, had published a book in which he traced one branch of it to a female slave of Thomas Jefferson. His family, of course, bought and destroyed every copy it could lay its hands on. Today, folks are much less touchy about such things, and many like to bring up some previous non-Aryan heritage of theirs.

To sum up, while I consider myself a true Spanish New Mexican—and no less a proud unhyphenated American who saw combat as a chaplain with our troops in World War II—I am always aware of whatever "restorations" from Native America had occurred down the lengthy course of almost four centuries. Nor do I feel inferior to any people from Spain, whether they be of higher class or mere peasants, who tend to look down, as the old British saying went, on the "colonials." At the same time I am so very proud of my New Mexico, the once miserable kingdom of my Chaves forebears, so beautiful in her adobe semblance as well as in her adobe memories which I kept recovering during a lifetime of casual research, while also prizing the recognition which critics both here and in England gave some of my poetry and prose written in their (*our*) precious language.[1]

By way of recapitulating this necessarily long ethno-historical Introduction, one can point out that the Chávez Clan of New Mexico is also most distinctive for leavening throughout her length and breadth so many of her old and newer families, whatever their surnames. Now, a recent "mitochondrial DNA" discovery claims that family names which are passed down by males eventually disappear, but that the genes passed on by the females can go on forever. According to this theory, ***while the merely external Chávez name was passed down by the sons bearing it, the basic family genes became ever more widespread through the Chávez women whose mates bore different surnames.***

1. In this country, a number of poems and short stories have kept appearing in anthologies and text-books, one tale making Foley's *The Best American Short Stories, 1948.*—In England, three poems were included in Moult's *Best Poems of the Year* (1938, 1940, 1941); another appeared in Alfred Noyes' *Golden Book of Catholic Poetry* (1946); *The Song of Francis*, a story of the saint first published here, was adopted for its own publication by the Sheldon Press (1978); and in 1958, T.S. Eliot strongly recommended *The Virgin of Port Lligat*, an ode with prose commentary, for a deluxe edition, which it got soon thereafter.

PART ONE

The First Progenitor

The Oñate Conquest of 1598-1600, by José Cisneros.

I. Don Pedro Gómez Durán y Chaves

Doña Isabel de Bohórques Vaca

1. Birth of a Poor Kingdom

Don Pedro Durán y Chaves finds first mention as such in 1602, as well as in all subsequent references to him. But he was not the very first Chaves in New Mexico. There were two others who had come in 1598 with Don Juan de Oñate's military entourage. One was the *alférez*[1] Diego Núñez de Chaves, thirty years old and a native of Guadalcanal near Llerena in Extremadura, who was killed at Ácoma when the ill-fated party of Oñate's Zaldívar nephew was massacred on that famous rock pueblo in December 1598. Another soldier, Alonso de Chaves, was one of the twenty-five who remained with the padre at San Gabriel when some colonists and friars deserted in 1601; not mentioned later, he must have returned to New Spain with his master Oñate.

As for Don Pedro Durán y Chaves, first mentioned as such in 1602 as just said, he had arrived in the second consignment of colonists and soldiers in 1600 as we discover later; also, that he was a native of Llerena like the officer killed at Ácoma. They could have been related in some way. By now a goodly number of the colonists of 1598 and 1600, disheartened by their abandonment during Oñate's mad searches all over for golden cities, were still clamoring for a return to New Spain. But Don Pedro and a *capitán*[2] named Cristóbal Vaca, who was his father-in-law or soon to be, and as heads of the opposing faction, wrote to the Viceroy proposing a continuation of the colony as a "*re publica*," as they put it, some sort of civil entity different from the military setup under Oñate. The province would then consist of a central capital and large grants of grazing land made to the people who stayed.

The Franciscan missionaries, however, prevailed upon the Spanish Crown to continue the colony as a back-up to their Indian mission enterprise, and for this they were assured material support from the royal treasury in Mexico City. And

1. Such terms are left untranslated for having different meanings than modern ones. *Alférez* (Arabic for ensign) was the lowest officer rank. *Alférez Real*, however, was a major coveted title for one who carried the Royal Ensign or Banner.

2. Such a captain (Latin for headman) meant the leader of any force, no matter how small. Its highest level was that of *Capitán-General*, applied only to the Governor, and from which the modern term "General" derives.

so Don Pedro's dream of a popular government died when in 1609 the land was formally constituted as *El Reyno de la Nueva Mēxico*, a baby kingdom no less, and calling for a proper capital city with a royal governor. In the following year, 1610, our Don Pedro levied a tax on certain freight brought up from Mexico City, civilian goods in the Mission supply caravan which also brought the kingdom's first royal governor, Don Pedro de Peralta.

Having accepted the new turn of events, Don Pedro assisted Governor Peralta in founding "*La Villa de Santa Fe de los Españoles*," as it was originally called.[3] A little *barrio* or ward was set aside for some volunteer servants from Tlascala who had come with the original colony; hence the place was called Analco (Aztec for "over the water," across the Santa Fe stream). These few superior-type Indians would gradually be replaced by lower-class *mestizos* and *mulatos* of every sort who came with the Mission supply trains of every three years, some of whom chose to stay in Analco. A few others of a more deleterious stripe, who arrived in the retinues of successive governors, also remained behind.[4]

Don Pedro next finds mention three years later, in 1613, referred to as a *capitān* trying to collect tribute from the Taos Indians for the same governor, but all in vain. For during the past three years, the infant kingdom had been wracked by serious crises brought on by none other than the head of the Franciscans, one Ordóñez by name, who claimed that his religious office superseded that of the civil ruler. He went so far as to have Governor Peralta kidnapped and put in chains; then he kept transferring his prisoner from one pueblo Mission to another to prevent his being rescued. But Peralta finally managed to escape by disguising himself as an Indian "*en cuero de Sībola*"—"in a hide from Cíbola." These and other such contentions which followed, but in which the ordinary Mission friars were usually the victims, could not help but most seriously affect all relationships between governors and missionaries throughout the rest of the century. Hence they also had to affect the ordinary colonists in their own relations with either of the two, not to mention the native Pueblo Indians with regard to all three categories.

As for Don Pedro Durán y Chaves, who is not mentioned with others involved

3. Not the "villa of St. Francis of Assisi," which came into use two centuries later, after 1823 when the City council chose St. Francis as patron saint.

4. *Mestizo* and other such terms as used in New Mexico are fully treated in a special section, pp. 184-89.

in the Ordóñez-Peralta affair, he could not help but form his own opinions in such matters, as we shall be seeing soon.

* * *

The above Peralta incident about a bison hide is brought up here and as a welcome break, for being the earliest reference we have concerning our peculiar New Mexican appellation, *cíbolo*, for that great animal. It shows how it developed from a people's confused historical memory, as so many accepted traditions usually do. Seventy-four years before, in 1539, the Indians far south in Sonora had trickily told Fray Marcos de Niza that the seven golden cities he sought were at a place called Cíbola much further north, and this name he had applied to the Zuñi pueblos he saw from afar. In the following year Coronado and his men, upon discovering that Niza's Cíbola consisted solely of mud villages, pressed onward looking for the golden cities out on the great plains in a mythical country called Quivira, again solely on the word of other wily Indians. This is when these Spaniards first saw the great herds of bison which they called *vacas corcovadas* (humped cattle), not knowing that they were similar to a closely related species, the bison, in the faraway northern frontiers of Poland and Russia.

And now, in Peralta's day, Cíbola had been transferred in the popular mind from Niza's Zuñi to Coronado's Quivira in the eastern plains; and since the correct Spanish term, *bisonte*, never reached them from Spain, they finally came to name these noble beasts *cíbolos*, and the hunters of them *ciboleros*. (In recent times a new county in western New Mexico was named Cíbola County, after its own Zuñi countryside which Fray Marcos had so named centuries before. But when asked by outside reporters where the name had originated, the common people told them it came from the female buffalo, once again twisting history around. But no less ignorant have been our English-speaking fellow citizens in the rest of the United States who have always misnamed the bison as "buffalo," which is a different kind of animal in the tropics.)

2. Troublous Times

This small but most apt title is borrowed from a work of the late Dr. France V. Scholes who was the prime historian on New Mexico's first century, and who admired the Chaves pioneers as "an independent lot" whom the governors often found it difficult to deal with. (While professor and dean at the University of New Mexico, he graciously volunteered to be my mentor when I first became interested in doing historical research.) As said earlier, Don Pedro Durán y Chaves finds no mention in those acrid fights between Governor Peralta and that pugnacious superior of the Franciscans. Nor had he been down in Acapulco around this time as I wrote long ago, mistaking him for a different Pedro de Chaves who became a high official in Manila and was dead by 1617.

But in the meantime our Don Pedro had been making up his mind about such church-state problems. Some of the governors who followed Peralta were outright scoundrels bent on exploiting Pueblo Indian labor, while a few of the persecuted Franciscans seemed to have no other purpose than to oppose the officials and relay the least bit of gossip to the Viceroy and the Inquisition in Mexico City. As a major official, Don Pedro finally became involved a decade later, in 1621, during the term of a really impious governor, Don Juan de Eulate. At Sandía on August 18, Padre Vergara wrote to the Inquisition, saying that Don Pedro de Chaves, while visiting the Tewa pueblos for Eulate, had publicly told the Indians not to obey the friars, "except for hearing their Mass," and not to take care of their livestock. On the same day Padre Haro of Nambé added his own complaint, saying that Don Pedro's sole aim was to "undo the missionaries" by what he told the Indians in their disfavor. Then on September 2 Padre Bautista of San Ildefonso appended his own accusation, claiming that Don Pedro had told the Indians "that in this land there was none other than one head, who was the governor, and him they were to obey."

These very same accusations were being repeated five years later, since a couple of bellicose friars could find no other such instances to bring up against him. At the same time one can see that Don Pedro had kept in mind that Peralta-Ordóñez squabble of ten years before, when he had determined that the civil officials and the missionaries should each stick to their own business. Then in 1624, as a *sargento mayor*,[5] he led a punitive expedition against the Jémez pueblos, whose medicinemen were plotting to eliminate the relatively few Spaniards of that early period. And so once again, in 1626, those very same accusations of 1621 were brought before the famed Fray Alonso Benavides, who had arrived in late

5. Not our modern "sergeant major," but an officer of field rank like our "major," this again a term derived from the former.

December of 1625 (when he brought the famed statue of La Conquistadora, subsequently writing his famous *Memorials* about New Mexico of 1630 and 1634). The infamous Governor Eulate was gone by this time, but some friars kept on recalling Don Pedro, and unjustly, as his bosom friend. Here, on April 11, 1626, Padre Zambrano of Galisteo recalled him as "an enemy of the Church" whom Eulate had sent to publish a decree among his Indians, to the effect that they "were not obliged to come and serve the church, nor their ministers, and when they rang for doctrine or Mass, only those should come who wished to hear it." Here one can see how much those original complaints of 1621 had intensified over the past five years.

And yet, the Inquisition down in Mexico City had taken no action, as it did in several other cases. Either the matter did not fall under its jurisdiction by way of blasphemy or heresy, or the several complaints based on that one single episode were not worth bothering about. By this time Don Pedro was also an *encomendero*, whereby the Indians of his district (around Sandía and San Felipe as we learn later) were "commended" to his care for their material well-being and their religious instruction, while he exacted tribute in goods from them for the central government and by way of a salary. This system of *encomiendas* had been abused so flagrantly down in southern New Spain that the poor natives there had become worse than slaves to their avaricious masters. In New Mexico it was altogether different, thanks to the influence which the friars had with the Crown, and also because the local *encomenderos* like Don Pedro harbored kinder feelings for their peaceful Indian subjects and close neighbors.

However, there were certain types of individuals who came with successive governors (and whom the padres referred to as evil *mestizos, pardos y amulatados*) who grossly misused and cruelly mistreated the poor Indians for their own ends, especially at the southern pueblos furthest away from Santa Fe. But no padre had ever accused Don Pedro or any other local *encomendero* of any such base misconduct.

On January 30 of this year of 1626, Don Pedro Durán y Chaves declared in Santa Fe that he was seventy years old and "one of the first settlers of this Villa and *maese de campo*[6] of these provinces." Then on May 22, Doña Isabel de Bohórques signed a testimony which identified her as "the wife of the *maese de*

6. "Field-master," similar to the field rank of colonel.

campo of these provinces, Pedro Durán y Chaves, inhabitants and founders of this Villa, forty years of age which she said herself to be, a little more or less." This was after she had been accused of saying five years before that the married state was superior to that of the celibate religious profession. (In a different complaint, she was said to have accused a certain Juan Gómez de Luna of "making unorthodox remarks," another example showing how much gossip was being spread about to bolster up any case meant for the Inquisition.) Her own signed deposition was in connection with those trite accusations being repeated against her husband, and the matter, as said before, was not pursued any further. On this same occasion she left for us a description of their family *estancia*[7] which will be treated later on when we look into her own background and her children.

As for her beloved husband, this is the last time we hear of him. He might have died later in this same year, or a few years after this incident.

3. *Story of a Noble Crest*

But nothing specific about the year of Don Pedro's arrival in New Mexico, or about his place of origin, seemed to have survived in the colonial records—until I came upon both by something like what we call serendipity, a lucky find as if by sheer chance. In his last will almost a century later, in 1707, his direct heir Don Fernando Durán y Chaves II listed his seven sons, the second of which he had named "Pedro" after his grandfather. But the very last of his ten children, and who was preceded also by three sisters, he also named "Peter" as *Pedro Gómez*. It was a most strange repetition of the Pedro name, and appended with a surname besides. This immediately stirred up in my memory one of Oñate's officers in the 1600 list of recruitments. He was the *Sargento Pedro Gómez Durán*, who was described as a well-built man of good features, fifty years old, the son of Hernán Sánchez Rico and a native of Valverde de Llerena in the jurisdiction of the Grand Master of Santiago.

Right away I began picturing the recruiting notary—whose script was awful as I recalled in the original document—putting down only what he pleased, as some such clerks happen to do even to this day. The well-accoutered fellow in the long line before him must have stated that he was the *Sargento Mayor Don Pedro*

7. A simple homestead including a grant of land. *Hacienda*, as used in Mexico, denoted a sumptuous residence overlooking a vast plantation, something which backward New Mexico never had.

Gómez Durān y Chaves, the son of Don Fernando Gómez Rico and a native of Valverde in the Magistracy of the military Order of Santiago. But this clerk, impatient with long names perhaps, while also hating high military rank and noble titles besides, put down only what first came to his head. His spelling of the father's first name was excusable, since Hernán is a shorter form of Hernando or Fernando, while writing Sánchez for Gómez showed careless attention—unless Sánchez happened to be a grandparental name which Don Pedro actually gave. As for the age of fifty, Don Pedro might have said so himself by way of a round number as was often done. For it is not too far off from the round age of seventy which he gave in 1626, his birth having occurred sometime between 1550 and 1556.

Also, considering his rather advanced age for those times, he might have had a previous wife back home in Spain, or else in Mexico City. All in all, my speculation fitted in perfectly with other information I already had, and all this was further confirmed later on by my own findings at Valverde de Llerena in Extremadura of southwestern Spain, and which in those times lay within the Magistracy of the knightly Order of Santiago.

* * *

Early in the past century, an outstanding New Mexican by the name of Manuel Antonio Chaves, later a Union lieutenant colonel during the Civil War, is said to have inherited two very old family heirlooms. One was a signet ring of pure gold bearing an escutcheon of five tiny keys; the other was a document telling about the origin of the Chaves name. Evidently, the ring had been passed from eldest son to eldest son down the past seven generations or so. As for the document, not a formal one, it might have been something copied from a book of heraldry in latter times; but how the colonel got it is a mystery, especially at a time of poor communication with a more sophisticated world outside.

This particular paper related that in the year 1160 two youths who were living in Portugal, Garcí and Ruí López by name, gathered an army on their own and with it wrested the Villa of Chaves from the Moors. For this feat King Alonzo Henríquez dubbed them both knights, giving them the Villa's name with a proper escutcheon. It also quoted an ancient inscription (in the mixed Portuguese and Castilian of that time and place) which existed inside the Chaves church:

Dos hermanos con ai quinas
sin rey ganaron a Chaves,
donde en Rouxo Cristalina
les hay dado por mas signas
en su escudo cinco llaves.

Translated: "Two brothers with eight quinas [*small silver shields of Portugal bearing five blue coins each*] won Chaves without any king's help, where on crystalline crimson they have been given, as additional emblems, five keys upon their escutcheon." This crest of five keys upon a crimson field, it went on to say, and orled or bordered with the royal *quinas* of Portugal, was still used by those of Trujillo. (Many years ago, Doña María Flora de Chaves, Duchess of Noblejas and head of the noble Chaves branch in Spain, told me that she still owned the traditional family *finca* or country home at Trujillo, and later sent me a hand-painted copy of the above-described crest which is here reproduced.)

As to how this Lady and I became acquainted, it bears telling. Her hobby it was to contact Chaves people anywhere in the world who had made a name for themselves, or at least made the news. I suspect that she had first contacted Senator Dennis Chávez in Washington because of his high position in the government of the United States, as Europeans regard the office, and then he had sent her my book on the *Origins of New Mexico Families*. Anyhow, I was completely surprised, and amused, by her first letter to me in which she stated that I was somehow very remotely related to her, and ending her greetings as "*su parienta*," your relative. I mischievously replied that any noble blood had long disappeared from my veins after four centuries of admixture with the humblest of folks. But this did not stop her from further correspondence in which she always ended her letters as my *parienta*.

Finally, when she happened to be in New York with her sister Doña Pilar, also a titled Lady who was visiting her daughter there, all three of them decided to fly to Santa Fe and so advised me by telegram. I met them at the small Santa Fe airport, and what impressed me most was what she said when we stepped outside in full view of the Sangre de Cristo panorama. "*Mira, Pilar*," she exclaimed to her sister, "*ésta es Castilla*!" This is Castile! She unwittingly had sown the seed in my head for the theme of a future book, *My Penitente Land*, which was published by the University of New Mexico.

Going back to that historical document, or paper, it went on to say that some other early Chaves descendants changed the color of the five keys to blue upon a field of gold, and with a crimson border bearing eight *aspas* (heraldic crosses).[8] These crosses of St. Andrew, it said, were added after a hero of the clan won fame in the crucial battle of Tolosa in the year 1212, as told by Don Luis Zapata de Chaves in his *Carlos Famoso*:

Son Chaves cinco llaves relucientes
en el hermoso escudo colorado,
su orla con ocho aspas excelentes
de San Andres el bienaventurado,
por los que antiguamente de sus gentes
fue el lugar de Baeza conquistado.

Translated: "Chaves are five shining keys on the beautiful red shield; its orle with eight outstanding crosses of the blessed Saint Andrew, whereby in ancient times the place of Baeza was conquered by its people."

As for the poet just quoted, we learn elsewhere that Don Luis Zapata de Chaves was a native of Llerena, and also the noted chronicler of Extremadura whose poetic narratives Cervantes did not think much of as literature. He was also a Knight of Santiago who was expelled from the Order because of certain romantic escapades of his. Of much more interest here, he was both a townsman and contemporary of our Don Pedro Durán y Chaves. (And so those St. Andrew's crosses he described give us a good excuse for employing the Scottish word "clan" in the title.)

The Duchess of Noblejas herself thought that the poet and our Don Pedro might have been kinsmen, which is very possible. This was after I told her that in our colonial records Don Pedro, as well as his sons and grandsons in that first century, were the only individuals, aside from the royal governors, to whom the title of *Don* was consistently applied by friend and foe alike. Then I playfully said to her: "Could my old ancestor Don Pedro have been a Knight of Santiago like his famed contemporary Don Luis Zapata de Chaves, and, like him, had been expelled from the Order for similar escapades, and for this reason had left Spain

8. The royal crest has the helmet facing forward. This knightly one, with five blue keys on gold, has it facing to the right for a legitimate ancestor, and to the left for a bastard one.

for the New World?'' The gentle Lady just looked chidingly at me for getting such a roguish idea.

Later on she sent me a copy, composed in her own hand, of her noble and regal family tree. It went back eight centuries to the time when one of the original Chaves sons married into the family of the later canonized San Fernando Rey, the first King of León and Castile. Hence he is the patron saint of this noble family descended from him. (She had also taken notice of the fact that ''Fernando'' had been the favorite given name of the early Chaves families of New Mexico.) Anyway, this good Lady's royal saintly ancestry did not deter some of us current Chávez commoners of New Mexico, with whatever remote Amerindian touches we may have, from starting a society as ''The Sons of San Fernando Rey.''

* * *

Now back to the New Mexico scene and the document just treated, as well as the signet ring connected with it. Early in this century, Don Amado Chaves, the son of that Col. Manuel Antonio treated before, related what he himself remembered as a lad. His father was then in command of a western American military post, later called Fort Wingate, when he made a trip to Albuquerque with his family, including the boy Amado. Somewhere near a place called Blue Water his carriage got mired in a flooded arroyo, and, when helping the driver to free the vehicle, the colonel lost the ring in the muddy current. As for the document's fate, there is no trace of it to my knowledge. Anyway, all of this clinches my serendipitous discovery of the identity and description of Don Pedro Gómez Durán y Chaves in 1600, as well as his place of origin. This last is supported by what I myself found in a trip to Spain years ago. In the city directories I seldom encountered the Chaves name, if at all. But when I came to the small city of Llerena and the village of Valverde close by, I found both places teeming with Chaves people (and one Chávez fellow from nearby Portugal), ordinary folks in the main who welcomed me like a relative who had been living abroad for some time. Hence I concluded—but did not tell them—that Extremadura had been drained of all her best Chaves males by the call of arms and adventure in a newly discovered world across the ocean sea.

4. *A Helpmate and Estancia*

This has been a long, if interesting, digression. Now back to Don Pedro Durán y Chaves, or rather his New Mexico family in particular. We have already reviewed his activities as found in the colonial records up to 1626, the year in which he might have died. Now we go back to that same testimony in this same year, the one signed by his wife, Doña Isabel de Bohórques. She began by mentioning a sister of hers called Doña Juana (de Zamora Vaca as we shall see). Here the clerk made it look as though she resided in Santa Fe, but she proceeded to tell that she and her husband had their *estancia* of El Tunque near the pueblo of San Felipe far to the south. Not that she stayed there all the time, but came up to the capital on occasion.

Some years before, after a good governor named Felipe Sotelo arrived in 1621, she had been invited by the *capitán* Francisco Gómez and his wife Doña Ana Robledo, herself a highly respected lady whose parents had come from Toledo, to stand with the governor himself as godparents for their eldest child. This Francisco Gómez, born in Portugal, was to escort Fray Alonso Benavides from Mexico City to Santa Fe four years later, in 1625, when the latter brought the La Conquistadora statue—his wife Doña Ana Robledo becoming the original promoter of its devotion and confraternity. Later, in 1641, when her husband was appointed as interim governor by a dying Governor Flores, some envious colonists accused him of being a *marrano* (secret Judaizer), and, after his demise, his eldest son Francisco had to defend his memory before the Inquisition in Mexico City. Here, more than thirty-five years later, Francisco Gómez Robledo—himself the earliest known *majordomo* of the Conquistadora Confraternity—was still boasting that Governor Sotelo and Doña Isabel de Bohórques, wife of the *maese de campo* Pedro de Chaves, had been his godparents in baptism.

Incidentally, the Judaic accusations against the junior Francisco's old father were that he always wore a cap (*yarmulke*) in the house, and on Fridays read Jewish books to his family; also, the boys had *colitas*, protruding tail-bones which the ignorant folks took as a sign of circumcision. To these charges he replied with humor, saying that the New Mexico mountain weather forced old men to wear caps at all times, and that his father taught his children letters lest they grow up as ignorant as other people; as for circumcision, he said, the old medic who examined him could see only a faint scar through his glasses!

A much younger brother of his, Andrés Gómez Robledo, was the only officer killed during the defense of Santa Fe at the outbreak of the Pueblo Revolt in 1680, and is brought up here to illustrate certain family admixtures already taking place within a very restricted Spanish population.[9] And this brings up my own intimate connection with the modern fortunes of the aforementioned statue of La Conquistadora. Formerly, the Santa Fe tradition held that the beloved image had been brought by Governor Don Diego de Vargas in 1692; but, as just shown, I discovered that it had come much earlier, in 1625, and that its devotion and confraternity had begun with that Gómez Robledo family. This was my first historical article published serially in the New Mexico Historical Review; and it also initiated my friendship with the great Dr. Sylvanus G. Morley who had it published in book form as *Our Lady of the Conquest*, with cover illustrations by the famed artist Jean Charlot. Meanwhile, I also had some ladies make dresses for the statue as described in the old documents; I also had a large carved chest made to hold the dresses and mantles. Then, for the Marian Year of 1954, I had the beloved Lady herself tell her story in *La Conquistadora: The Autobiography of an Ancient Statue*, dedicating it to those Gómez Robledo ancestors on both my parents' sides. Some years later, I had her 1717 chapel authentically restored, adding as a fitting throne a reredos made from two 1730 altarpieces which had survived, covered with white enamel, as side altars in the Cathedral.

All of this has practically been forgotten by a new generation, but a wonderful caption to it all occurred in September of 1987 when King Juan Carlos and Queen Sofia of Spain visited Santa Fe for a single day. Local officialdom had filled it out with purely social events, but the king insisted on visiting the cathedral that afternoon. Apprised beforehand, our good Archbishop Sánchez met their Majesties at the main entrance and then led them straight to the Conquistadora chapel where he had me address them briefly on both the statue and the chapel. They both smiled graciously when I ended by saying that New Mexico's La Conquistadora was not a Virgin of miracles as in other places, but rather a beloved *paisana* of ours, just like the Sagrario Virgin of Toledo and the Guadalupe Virgin of Extremadura whence her very first devotees had come.

9. GENEALOGY: *a*) **Francisco Gómez**, Andrés Gómez Robledo, Francisca Gómez Robledo, Ambrosio Mariano Roybal, Juan Manuel Roybal, Romualdo Roybal, Nicolasa Roybal, Fr. A. Chávez.—*b*) **Francisca Gómez Robledo**, María Roybal, Juliana Archibéque, Miguel Gabaldón, Toribio Luna, María Encarnación Luna, Eugenio Chávez, Fabián Chávez, Fr. A. Chávez.

* * *

Going back to Don Pedro de Chaves and his wife Doña Isabel, both of them stood as witnesses, on January 16, 1622, for the marriage in Santa Fe of one Diego de Vera, a newcomer from the Canary Islands, and María de Abendaño. This bride was Doña Isabel's own niece, the daughter of a Simón de Abendaño and her younger sister María Ortiz Vaca, both of them already deceased. This couple, or their daughters rather, will come into play in a most colorful drama decades later in connection with a certain Chaves maternal line, and which is here cited for the same reasons as the preceding footnote.[10]

As for Don Pedro's *estancia* called "El Tunque," this is the Indian name for a very wide and dry arroyo running down from the present Ortiz range in the east to join the Rio Grande near San Felipe Pueblo. From its full length the property, bounded on the west by the river, spread southward to the Indian lands belonging to the Tiwa pueblos of Puaray and Sandía. All this, together with the vast area with other settlers' homesteads where Albuquerque is now, was called the *Alcaldía* of Sandía.[11] Also, at the upper eastern reaches of the Tunque arroyo, there was a small Indian settlement called San Pedro, evidently so named by Don Pedro after his name-saint as have other places ever since. It was the home of a few Tiwa families from nearby Puaray living on or near the buried ruins of a prehistoric pueblo which archaeologists have unearthed and investigated, calling it Paa-ko. (San Pedro was also the name of a much more recent mining town, recently defunct, in the general vicinity just north of the Paa-ko ruins. This means, as it happened in other instances in local history, that the name San Pedro had been passed down the centuries in popular tradition.)

The actual residence of Don Pedro and Doña Isabel stood by the river in the fertile area now owned by the Santa Ana Indians and called Ranchos de Santa Ana. This we learn from Don Pedro's grandson, Don Fernando the Second, who inherited the property by right of primogeniture, and called it Bernalillo after his own firstborn son. It is here that Doña Isabel de Bohórques reared her children while her husband was either politicking in Santa Fe or out on a military cam-

10. GENEALOGY: **Diego de Vera**, María de Vera, Luisa Montoya, Bernardina de Salas, Lucía Hurtado, Antonio Chaves, Cristóbal Chaves, José Mariano Chaves, José Encarnación Chaves, José Francisco Chaves, Eugenio Chávez, Fabián Chávez, Fr. A. Chávez.

11. A territorial division headed by an *alcalde* (Arabic for chief). The *alcalde mayor* was a town's chief executive, whence our modern term "mayor."

paign. And so, of course, she deserves equal treatment with her husband, and no less because in family lines the wife and mother with her own family background is just as important as the sire and his own; after all, she is the one who carries the burden of bearing and rearing.

Both her family and Don Pedro Durán y Chaves had come in the same contingent of 1600, and he could have married her soon thereafter, or else in the year following. As pointed out long before, it is quite possible that he had lost a first wife in Spain or in Mexico City, from the fact that he was between forty-five and fifty at the time. As for herself, she was about sixteen or so when they married, based on her statement in 1626 about being forty years old, "more or less." Many years ago I had tried to connect her with some Bohórques men, with one of whom Don Pedro had been briefly associated, but they turned out to be transients, or else involved in some Inquisition case without ever having been in New Mexico. What led me to her own family's identity was a statement that Don Pedro himself made, that he was the brother-in-law of an Antonio Vaca.

This man's family in the 1600 recruitment list was described as follows: The *capitán* Cristóbal Vaca, the son of Juan Vaca, being of good stature with a dark complexion and good features, and thirty years old. His wife was Ana Ortiz, the daughter of Francisco Pacheco. With them were three grown girls named Juana de Zamora, Isabel (de Bohórques as we learn later), María de Villarubia (more like Villanueva in the original bad script), and a small boy named Antonio. Both the parents and their children were natives of Mexico City. The first girl, Juana, married a Simón Pérez de Bustillo, and the third one a Simón de Abendaño as we have already seen. As for the varied surnames which the daughters had, it was a customary harking back to those of grandparents on either side, a most perplexing practice of those times which makes it impossible for one to establish relationships without other supporting evidence. What also seems quite possible, the three grown-up daughters could have been Vaca's children by a previous wife, while the much younger boy Antonio (and other children to come) were by Ana Ortiz Pacheco.

Also to be noted is the fact that, unlike the then restricted *Don* title for men, *Doña* in those times was accorded the wives of some of the more prominent colonists. Things would be different in the following century when both *Don* and *Doña* came to be applied to men and women who were outstanding in their respective communities, or else had reached a respectable old age.

The surname of Doña Isabel's father also merits treatment like the one of her Chaves husband. It was a shortening of Cabeza de Vaca (Cow's Head), an equally historic surname which went far back to the already romanticized Moorish Wars in Spain. It had been bestowed upon a farmer or herdsman who marked a strategic river ford with a cow's skull, thus enabling a Spanish king to cross over with his troops and surprise the Moorish enemy. Centuries later a descendant with this long name became famous for having taken away the Canary Islands from the French. And in the New World we have a much better known descendant, Álvar Núñez Cabeza de Vaca, still famous for his narrative of the marvelous things he experienced among the Indians between Florida and what is now northern Texas. But the name had already been reduced by some to plain Vaca when Cortés conquered the Aztec City of Mexico, there being some such individuals among his soldiers. Hence Doña Isabel's own grandfather, Juan de Vaca, could have been a son of one of those men (and by some Aztec belle perhaps).

But in New Mexico, Vaca was soon being spelled "Baca." This was not out of pure ignorance, as some might think, but from a labial quirk in Spanish as it is spoken. Two thousand or so years ago, the great Seneca, who had been born and reared in Spain, told his fellow Romans that for the Spaniards the verb *vívere* (to live) was the same as *bíbere* (to drink). A most clever pun it was, but also illustrating for us how it was so natural for Vaca to become Baca.

* * *

For Doña Isabel de Bohórques Vaca to have managed a large homestead such as El Tunque, with such vast grazing grounds and its farmland besides, a number of herders and laborers had been altogether necessary. These Don Pedro had provided with some *mestizos* and *mulatos* which are also mentioned in her statement, one of whom had married an Indian woman of San Felipe. Don Pedro, no doubt, had picked them up at Analco in Santa Fe. But the cream of her *estancia*'s crop, she would have told anyone, were her two staunch sons, Don Fernando and Don Pedro the Younger. There was also a daughter, a junior Isabel, who will be alluded to later on. (Most likely there was a third son, referred to as Don Agustín, who was a contemporary of these two but about whom we know almost nothing.)

Here we can see that Don Pedro who, like other *conquistadores*, bore his maternal surname of Durán y Chaves, had named his firstborn son after his own father, Fernando Gómez and the second one after himself. Now to what the records tell us about the two sons and about their own immediate descendants.

Imaginary map of New Mexico by Sanson d'Abbeville, 1657.
Courtesy, Museum of New Mexico.

II. Don Fernando Durán y Chaves I

Doña María Carvajal Holguín

1. The Miserable Kingdom

Once referred to as "the eldest son of his father," Don Fernando, as the first-born son that he was, inherited Don Pedro's *estancia* of El Tunque and his *encomienda*. We find first mention of him in 1638 when, as a resident of the Sandía *Alcaldía*, he had also been chosen as the *teniente de gobernador*[1] for the Río Abajo, all of the Rio Grande country south of Santa Fe. This is when he testified that he had returned from an expedition to the Apotlapihuas (enroute to Santa Fe?) with Governor Luis de Rosas. Now, this very governor, who turned out to be as villainous and lecherous as one can imagine, brings us to the sad colonial state of affairs which existed in Don Fernando's day. It had become steadily worse than the one his father Don Pedro had experienced.

That Ordóñez-Peralta crisis was a thing of the past, as well as the Eulate one which followed, but the good friars kept on being harassed for defending their Mission Indians, and here the majority of the original colonists faithfully sided with them. And now a string of governors being sent from Mexico City, like this Rosas and three successive ones named Manso, Mendizábal and Peñalosa, were nothing but scoundrels with high-sounding backgrounds whose sole aim was to exploit the padres and their Pueblo Indian people, as well as any of the colonists who openly opposed them on this score.

Later in this same year of 1638, Don Fernando signed a complaint, this time as a *capitán*, against Rosa's abuses of every sort. These continued until January 25, 1642, when several irate colonial leaders and others—his uncle Antonio Baca among them—went and murdered the evil fellow for his crimes. The actual assassin was a soldier named Nicolás Ortiz, a late-comer who had married a niece of Antonio Baca. Governor Rosas had seduced her and made her pregnant while her husband was away with the supply-train between Santa Fe and Mexico City. This Ortiz was immediately tried and found guilty, and then was sent down to Mexico City for a final disposition of his case. However, as months went by, rumor had it that Don Fernando Durán y Chaves and some others, including his brother-

1. Not our "lieutenant governor" with his rights of office, but simply the governor's temporary representative at the Río Abajo area well removed from the Capital.

in-law Agustín de Carvajal, had been part of the cabal. And so in 1643, when a new governor arrived in the person of Don Alonso Pacheco de Herédia, orders were issued for the arrest of "Don Fernando de Chaves [*and twelve others*], condemned to death as traitors for their flight and crimes."

But only eight men, his uncle Antonio Baca among them, were arrested and then beheaded in Santa Fe on July 21, 1643. (*Degollados* meant slitting the throat all the way instead of chopping the head off as in other lands.) But Chaves, Carvajal, and others, including Alonso Baca (the executed Antonio's younger brother) were spared, receiving official pardon the following day. This pardon came, it was said, because Don Fernando and some others had attended the execution; in fact he was confirmed as the *alcalde* of Sandía. Another version has it that the sentence of all the original suspects had at first been delayed for fourteen days on the plea of Fray Juan de Salas of the southern Cuarác Mission, where all the suspects must have fled. It was with the proviso that they return to their domestic affairs within that period, after which they were to receive a general pardon. (Many years ago, mistaking the above incident for two separate ones, I blamed Governor Pacheco for finally turning against Don Fernando after that pardon. The fact that he had paid attention to Padre Salas' plea shows that he had some respect for the friars—or had he used it as a trick to get the suspects back?)

In any case, Don Fernando and some others were exonerated after what seems to have been a fair trial. The execution of those other eight men was obviously meant to set an example for anyone harboring similar ideas. Nor was it forgotten. It is while recalling this incident a generation later that Don Fernando's son, Fernando the Younger, called his New Mexico a "miserable kingdom," an expression still later used by one of his sons.

In the following year, on August 17, 1644, Don Fernando declared that he had been born in New Mexico and was thirty-five years old, while his younger brother Pedro was thirty-three. This would place their respective births around the years 1609 and 1611, rather late if their parents had been married shortly after 1600 as we have supposed. Even so they could have been preceded by their sister Isabel, or by some children who had died in infancy, which was a common occurrence in those difficult times. Whatever, people were always giving wrong or conflicting ages, since the annual calendars we take for granted did not exist in those days. Two years later, in 1646, we find Don Fernando Durán y Chaves and Don Agustín de Chaves in a military escort which conducted a new governor, Don Luis de Guzmán, from Mexico City to Santa Fe. Why they had traveled there in the first place we have no way of knowing; perhaps they had escorted his predecessor, Don Fernando de Arguello, back home. (As for the aforesaid Don Agustín, I had previously presumed that he was Don Fernando's eldest son, but his age precludes this and so he could have been his younger brother.)

From what we know from the extant records, no Chaves individual seems to have been involved in further plots or crises during the next fourteen years. There is a dearth of documentation for this period, or else the governors during this time could have been more decent fellows. But in 1660 and 1661 we find Don Fernando's signature under complaints criticizing a subsequent governor by the name of Bernardo López de Mendizábal. Here he signed as a *sargento mayor*. This Mendizábal had been creating quite a stir, not only by his persecution of friars and colonists alike, but by blasphemous and unorthodox declarations in connection with debaucheries at governmental headquarters in which his wife was also involved. In 1662 Don Fernando was accused of having talked against the governor with Fray Alonso de Posada, the *Custodio* or head of the Franciscan Missions, as they rode up from the southern Mission of Senecú (the Socorro area) to Sandía. But soon, after a slew of accusations had reached the Inquisition in Mexico City, Mendizábal was recalled to answer for all his excesses.

Then he was succeeded by just as infamous a governor, Diego de Peñalosa, during whose term a most interesting episode occurred which involved three Chaves men. Because of his alliance with the friars, Don Fernando had been put in prison at the *casas reales*.[2] Then the governor ordered the arrest of his brother Pedro, as well as Don Fernando's own son, named Cristóbal. For this he sent down an armed guard to the southern half of the Sandía *Alcaldía* to fetch Don Pedro and his nephew Don Cristóbal who was living there with him. This was during August of 1663, when the guards with their two prisoners stopped overnight at the pueblo of Santo Domingo, which happened to be the headquarters of the Franciscan Custody. That same night Don Pedro had an Indian carry him into the mission church, from where he began claiming the right of sanctuary the next day. But Peñalosa had no scruples about violating that right, and ordered both men to be brought up to Santa Fe. He also imprisoned Fray Alonso de Posada, the *Custodio* stationed there.

2. "Royal houses," or gubernatorial residence and headquarters, now called The Palace of the Governors.

How all of them came to be freed is best left for the sections on Don Pedro II and the younger Don Cristóbal. In the meantime down in Mexico City, ex-governor Mendizábal, on trial before the Inquisition, was falsely claiming that Don Fernando de Chaves had forewarned him about the friars' meddling in his *residencia*, the accounting of his term as governor! And it was during this acrimonious period that other people had been moving into his Tunque *estancia* during the terms of Mendizábal and Peñalosa, both of whom he had offended by siding with the missionaries. The extreme eastern area of the already abandoned tiny pueblo of San Pedro had been granted to a Diego de Montoya, while much closer to his place of residence, at a spot being called Angostura, other individuals had moved in. These last will be met with years later under the most dramatic circumstances.

All the while, Don Fernando had continued siding with his Franciscan friends. By April 1, 1669, he was referred to as dead by Fray Juan Bernal, a most zealous padre (and future martyr) who ruefully mentioned this in a letter of this date to the Holy Office of the Inquisition. The year before, 1668, Don Fernando had led an expedition against the Indians of the plains, hence he might have perished during that campaign.

2. His Helpmate and Estancia

Now to his wife, as we did for his mother Doña Isabel de Bohórques, but with precious little to go on. In fact, we do not even have her given name. She must have always stayed down at El Tunque, away from the social and political turmoil in Santa Fe, that she finds no mention in the records. Only once was she referred to indirectly when Agustín de Carvajal, the man associated with her husband Don Fernando in the Rosas murder affair, was identified as being his brother-in-law. Hence she was a Carvajal, and whom we now christen "María," this name implied by long Spanish custom as the first part of almost every girl's baptismal name. As Agustin's sister, she was then the daughter of one of Don Juan de Oñate's favorite men, Juan de Vitoria Carvajal, who had come to New Mexico in his entourage of 1598. And so we have a great deal about her family background as for Don Fernando's own mother Isabel.

Juan de Vitoria Carvajal was described in the 1598 lists as an *alférez* thirty-seven years old, the son of Juan de Carvajal and born at Ayotepel in the Marquisate of the Valley (of Mexico). He was of medium stature and wore a chestnut beard. His surname had been a most prominent one down there since the Cortés Conquest, and one can see him hinting at some superior ancestry by specifying his birthplace's association with Cortés' title of *marqués*. Among the latter's men there had been an Antonio Carvajal from Zamora in Spain, and the ancestry of a Luis de Carvajal was linked with that of his present leader, Don Juan de Oñate. (There was also a younger officer with exactly the same long name, but having a different father, Alonso Ruíz de Guzmán. The two could have been first cousins, both bearing their grandparental name of Vitoria. It is not known if this man had any family, or if he stayed in New Mexico. In 1609 he escorted Governor Peralta to Santa Fe, and he finds last mention in 1617 as an *alférez* thirty years old in association with the older Vitoria Carvajal, a *capitán* at the time and fifty-five years of age.)

As for this older Carvajal, he had always enjoyed Oñate's trust, who had sent him back to New Spain to bring the second colonial batch of colonists in 1600, the one in which Don Pedro Durán y Chaves came, as well as his wife's Vaca family. Here Carvajal was again described as formerly, with the added notation that he was well-featured, and having a mark above his left eye. While he was the *alcalde mayor* of Santa Fe in 1614, he was accused by others of having illegally assumed authority when he ordered an Indian assassin executed while Governor Peralta was in prison (during the Ordóñez affair of the previous year). Then in 1622 he was mentioned as the *síndico* of the Franciscans, their term for the layman who handled their material affairs. Here he referred to himself as a married man and a "first founder of the land." In 1629, as the *Alférez Real* for the Holy Office, he accompanied Padre Perea, a really fine *Custodio* of the friars, in a memorable procession which went out of Santa Fe to welcome an incoming new lord governor, Don Francisco Nieto de Silva.

Sometime after 1600, Carvajal had married an *Isabel Holguín*, who herself could boast of no mean background. Her father, Juan López Holguín, was also an *alférez* when he came in 1600 with his wife and family. The latter's name was Catarina de Villanueva, who, like some housewives of her day, dabbled in home-remedies for lack of physicians and the like. (In 1626 local gossip accused her of trafficking in "magic roots.") López Holguín himself had been described as being of good stature and black-bearded with a scar over one eye, and forty years old, the son of Juan López Villasana and a native of Fuente Ovejuna in

Extremadura. (This town, which I purposely visited, lies not far east from Valverde de Llerena, hence López Holguín and Don Pedro Durán y Chaves must have often exchanged reminiscences of their native Extremadura.) Nothing else is known about him save that in 1626, when he gave his age as forty-six, he reminded others that he was a "founder of the kingdom."

His eldest son, Simón, went by the name of Abendaño, evidently his child by a previous wife in Spain, since he gave Ciudad Rodrigo as his birthplace; he had then married María Ortiz, a daughter of Cristóbal Vaca, and both were dead by 1622. Their only known child, María de Abendaño, married a Diego de Vera in this same year, with Governor Sotelo and Doña Isabel de Bohórques standing as witnesses as we have already seen. A younger son was Cristóbal Holguín. And then there was the Isabel Holguín who became the wife of Juan de Vitoria Carvajal.

* * *

As for our dear Doña "María" Carvajal Holguín, about whose person we know nothing else—not even her first name—and whom Don Fernando presumably left a widow in 1668 or 1669, she had given him one son whom we know from the documents. She had named him Cristóbal after her own brother or else Don Fernando had done so after his own maternal Vaca grandfather. Yet there had to be another younger son whom Don Fernando named after his Chaves grandfather and after himself. This must await clarification when this junior Fernando's time comes. As for that Don Agustín de Chaves who most likely was Don Fernando's younger brother, we find him mentioned only twice: in 1646 when he and Don Fernando were in the military escort which brought Governor Guzmán to New Mexico, and then in 1665 when, for whatever reason, he went far down to Parral and appears no longer in the records. Now to the one son just mentioned.

3. *A Wayward Son*

Don Cristóbal Durán y Chaves, the son of Don Fernando and his Carvajal wife, finds first mention in 1663 when he was living further south from his father's estate with his uncle Don Pedro II, and was arrested with the latter by Governor Peñalosa. That incident had already been told, when his uncle sought sanctuary in the Santo Domingo mission church, and when both were nevertheless brought up to Santa Fe. What has not been told is that they were released with a full pardon through the influence of a fellow named Tomé Domínguez de Mendoza, who was Don Pedro's brother-in-law as well as the young Cristóbal's affianced father-in-law. At this time Cristóbal had stated that he was still single, twenty-four years old, and a resident of the Sandía district. In the following year he said that he was twenty-five and already married to *Juana Domínguez de Mendoza*, daughter of that same Tomé and his wife Catarina López Mederos.

The last thing we know about this Don Cristóbal occurred three years later, in 1667, when he was accused of pulling a dagger on a certain friar who had been writing satires about certain colonists—no doubt his several Domínguez de Mendoza in-laws when we consider their characters and background. Nor is he listed among the refugees of 1680, following the Pueblo Revolt of that year, having either died or been summoned down to Mexico City.

Here the entire Domínguez de Mendoza family must be briefly reviewed because of the baneful influence its members had on the New Mexico colony at large, and in particular on the majority of their Chaves contemporaries. All natives of Mexico City, and a most vigorous and gifted bunch to say the least, they had come in 1661 in the entourage and household of that infamous Governor Peñalosa. Their maternal aunt, Juana de la Cruz y Mendoza, was Peñalosa's housekeeper, while her son, Luis de Ulloa, was the governor's personal page. Their own mother, Elena Ramírez de Mendoza, who also came along with her grown family, was the widow of the senior Tomé Domínguez who had died down in Mexico City at the age of ninety-six around the year 1656. Now she had brought along three adult sons and four daughters. These sons, Tomé, Juan, and Francisco, were soon engaged in trading native goods such as wool and hides with merchants far south in northern New Spain.

One girl, Elena, soon married Don Pedro Durán y Chaves II as we have seen. The eldest son, Tomé *el Mozo* (the Younger) had also brought his wife Catarina López Mederos and their family, among whom was their daughter Juana who three years later married this young Don Cristóbal Durán y Chaves. Moreover, his aunt, sister of his father Don Fernando I and of his uncle Don Pedro II, and who used the full name of Doña Isabel Durán de Chaves y Bohórques, became the wife of Tomé's younger brother, Juan Domínguez de Mendoza. This latter pair is known to have had two daughters, María D. de Mendoza who married Diego Lucero de Godoy, and an anonymous one who was the wife of Diego de Hinojos.

As just said, it was this Tomé Domínguez de Mendoza who had gotten his patron Peñalosa to pardon his brother-in-law and future son-in-law following that Santo Domingo sanctuary episode. As henchmen of that same impious governor, Tomé and his two brothers must have been riling the friars to such a point as to cause one of them to compose those satires which made Don Cristóbal threaten him with his dagger. So much unlike his father Don Fernando, who had always been such a staunch friend of the Franciscans, he had become their bitter foe through his marital and mercenary connections with the Domínguez de Mendozas. What also appears to have been the case, Don Fernando had severed all fraternal relations with his younger brother Pedro and his sister Isabel for these very same reasons. Had he also disowned his own son Cristóbal who had left the paternal home to live with his uncle Don Pedro D. y Chaves and his carnal aunt Doña Isabel?

As mentioned before, Cristóbal might have died well before the 1680 Pueblo Revolt since he does not appear among the refuges at El Paso del Norte where his uncle and aunt with the Domínguez in-laws continued profiteering, and this brings us to a full treatment of Don Fernando's younger brother.

III. Don Pedro Durán y Chaves II

Elena Domínguez de Mendoza

1. A Stain on the Escutcheon

Unlike his elder brother Don Fernando, this second Don Pedro was not that much of an enviable character. Following the Pueblo Revolt of 1680—to be treated shortly in fullest detail because of its great importance in local annals—his fellow refugees down at El Paso del Norte were complaining that he was taking advantage of their misery by grabbing an undue share of the relief which had been sent up from Mexico City, and trading with it for his own profit besides. He had given his age as seventy in 1680, declaring one son old enough to bear arms, ten minor children, and thirty servants. One aged critic stated that far back in 1637 he was still living with his mother (Doña Isabel de Bohórques), which indicated that his father Don Pedro the First had passed away well before that date. He was still single at the time, and perhaps had married for the first time shortly thereafter. All that we know is that sometime after 1661 he was married to *Elena Domínguez de Mendoza* as previously related. (His sister Isabel D. y Chaves, as shown before, was the wife of Elena's brother Juan Domínguez de Mendoza.)

At this very time he was boasting that he had served his Majesty even without having an *encomienda* (since his elder brother Don Fernando had inherited it), and that his (Chaves and Vaca) grandparents had been among "the first *conquistadores* of the Kingdom," and also that his own father Don Pedro "and those others had ended their lives in the royal service." But before he could get started on his own record, some refugees contended that he had indeed been connected with three military campaigns led by his uncle Antonio Baca, that is, by paying a certain Pascual Naranjo to take his place in one of them, and likewise a José Padilla in another. Here he was also accused of having been one of those masked men who had accompanied Nicolás Ortiz when the latter murdered Governor Rosas back in 1642, and that for his complicity he had been banished to Mexico City by Governor Guzmán. (But this did not fit in with his craven character, and moreover the accusation was untrue; for we know that those masked men had been executed in 1643, and that Governor Guzmán had not arrived until several years later.)

As for that right of sanctuary incident twenty years afterward, in 1663, when he and his nephew Don Cristóbal were arrested by Governor Peñalosa and he had taken refuge in the Santo Domingo church, it had been a dispute over livestock and not any high principle. And then they had been set free through the influence of Tomé Domínquez de Mendoza, a lackey of the tyrant governor as we have seen. This was not only because Don Pedro was already married to Tomé's sister Elena, while his nephew was scheduled to marry Tomé's daughter Juana, but because all of them were engaged in the livestock and textile export business with Casas Grandes and San Felipe de Jesús (later called Chihuahua) far down in New Spain.

Back in 1667, this Don Pedro had declared that he had been born in Santa Fe and was forty years old—a far cry from his age of thirty-three given by his elder brother in 1644, but closer to his own estimate of seventy in 1680. Here he also declared that his own *estancia* (granted by Peñalosa most likely) lay four leagues north of Isleta Pueblo, that is, on the west bank of the Rio Grande in the general area called Atrisco (from Aztec *Atlixco* meaning "across the river"). This name was obviously applied to it by *mestizos* from Santa Fe's Analco who were servants of a Pedro Varela de Losada whose *estancia* (now Los Barelas) lay on the east bank. Centuries later Atrisco was still being remembered as the grant made to Pedro Durán y Chaves.

Now to that momentous event which has served as the basis for this introduction.

2. The Pueblo Revolt of 1680

It was a great fiasco, to say the least, one which most radically altered the history of *El Reyno de la Nueva México*, and no less the fortunes and subsequent make-up of her Chaves clan. It has to be quite thoroughly reviewed here, not merely for the instruction of our Chaves and other descendants of New Mexico's first settlers, but because it has been written about by outsiders with a definite anti-Spanish and anti-Catholic bias which goes far back to the English so-called Black Legend about Spain.

On August 10, 1680, the feast of San Lorenzo, twenty-one Franciscans were killed at their scattered mission stations, along with any of the colonists living close to some pueblos, some of them stationed there as overseers. At the *Alcaldía* of Santa Fe, which included the *estancias* of La Cañada north of the capital and those of Los Cerrillos south of it, their people had taken refuge with Santa Fe's inhabitants. There they were to endure a two-week siege. There were no Chaves folk among them, since all of these resided much further south in the Río Abajo. But at their *Alcaldía* of Sandía, in the northwest corner of the Chaves *estancia* of El Tunque, three non-Chaves families living at a spot called Angostura were massacred by warriors from the pueblo of Santo Domingo.

The one Chaves family living in the ancestral homestead just south of Angostura would also have been wiped out, were it not for the fact that the Rio Grande just below this point had changed its course some indefinite time before, leaving it on its west bank. This was the family of a younger Don Fernando Durán y Chaves with his wife and four small children, whose full story will be told in the next major section. They barely managed to escape further south to join the already alarmed families, many of them related by blood or marriage, both in the Sandía and Isleta *alcaldías* where the Indians of these pueblos had not joined the revolt as yet.

Presuming that all of the colonists of Santa Fe and points north had already been exterminated, the *capitán* Alonso García, who happened to be the *teniente de gobernador* for the Río Abajo at the time, decided to abandon the land and seek refuge more than a hundred leagues south at the Guadalupe Mission and settlement of El Paso del Norte. This Mission and town had been founded some two decades before by a friar from the southern New Mexico Mission of Socorro, and the first Spanish families sent there to offer him protection were all from New Mexico as well. And so the present refugees would be joining old acquaintances, even relatives. At the southernmost *Alcaldía* of Senecú, which included the Piro pueblos of Senecú and Socorro, they were joined by the colonists living in that area, as well as by the friendly, christianized Piros of those two pueblos.

By this time, and unbeknownst to them, the soldiers and citizens at Santa Fe, under the current Governor Don Antonio de Otermín, had finally managed to break the siege temporarily, which gave them enough time to escape south with all their people. They caught up with the Río Abajo refugees well before these reached El Paso del Norte, when the *teniente* Alonso García and the men of his fleeing party were soundly blamed for having abandoned their fellow-colonists of the capital. And one can hardly blame the governor for not accepting their excuses, for it all had indeed been a most sad and fatal blow, not only to the Franciscan Missions and their many padres who had lost their lives, but to a Spanish colony and "kingdom" which had managed to exist—however so poorly and precariously—for more than eight decades.

* * *

Nor was it less a howling success and great triumph for the original inhabitants of the land, or rather for their religious leaders. Our eastern and other American brethren are always calling the event a patriotic Native American victory for national freedom, as if such modern republican or democratic ideas existed in those times, particularly among a primitive people. Imbued with the old English "Black Legend" regarding Spain and anything Spanish, and which refuses to die, they persist in writing that it was the typically Spanish cruel enslavement of the Indians which had made them rise up in patriotic protest. It is true, as we have been seeing all along, that certain royal governors, and those *mestizo* henchmen they brought with them, had on occasion enslaved or tried to enslave some of the helpless people of the pueblos. But the friars had always stood up to them as "Protectors of the Indians," which they were by royal decree, all of which we learn from what they wrote repeatedly to the Viceroy and the Inquisition. As for the colonial leaders, like our Chaves and other ancestors, they, too, had gotten into serious trouble with those evil governors for siding with the friars and their Mission Indians.

No doubt, many an Indian remembered such base mistreatment, whether personally or from stories passed down from many years back in each pueblo. However, the real cause of the Pueblo Revolt was what can be called a "religious one," not in the sense of a popular uprising as in the one of the native religious leaders striving to keep themselves in complete power. This is nothing new. It goes back all the way from more recent Christian eras to older Hebraic ones in Scripture, and still further beyond to more ancient pagan days, when the high priests of whatever forms of worship they had got their monarchs to wage wars in order to preserve their hieratic turf along with theirs.

Here, for eighty-two years now, the Franciscans had been weaning away, if ever so slowly, many of the ordinary pueblo folk from their old traditional beliefs to accept Christian ones, if ever so imperfectly. Yet all this was enough to weaken their *caciques'* complete hold on their daily lives. (*Cacique*, meaning "headman," was an Aztec term generally applied to them by the Spaniards, although they also called them *hechiceros*, male witches or warlocks.) These medicinemen, to use a popular English term, cherished the "know-how" of their "Ancient Ones" (supernal beings of some sort), whereby they supervised every phase of daily life in their particular villages through complicated rituals of dances, fetish worship, and the like.

On the friars' part, these dispensers of the Spanish King's bounty had brought the people many material benefits they had never known before, and which helped the friars in their so-called conversions. Their triennial Mission supply caravans had brought them new kinds of seeds for sowing, domestic animals like sheep and goats for breeding, and—most wonderful of all—metal tools and all-purpose knives which were miracles to folks living in the Stone Age. These the friars gave to each pueblo's *governor* (a civic office the Spaniards introduced, ceremonial cane and all), for them to distribute among their subjects in return for work done. This is how those friars induced them to build such imposing churches with their attached *conventos*, and not by military force as some bigots have written in the past. Naturally, the *caciques* resented all this, and it is reflected in what some Indians told the Spaniards when these returned after the rebellion; namely, that their medicinemen had told the people, besides having to wash off their baptisms in the rivers, to desecrate the churches and to destroy all foreign seeds except those of "beans and squashes" which they had always had.

But what had brought the medicinemen's anger to a peak in recent years was the fanaticism of certain new friars who got the military to destroy their *estufas* (now called *kivas*) for being temples of the devil. They also had some people punished for participating in dances and other native rituals which they considered witchcraft and idolatry, but which former milder friars had tolerated as a harmless part of their native culture. On the civil side, there were old memories of cruelties inflicted by this or that Spanish governor's lackeys in the past, as we have seen. And not the least was the hanging, not too many years before, of some *caciques* at a couple of pueblos who had foolishly thought that their few subjects alone were strong enough to wipe out the Spaniards along with the missionaries.

Therefore, a united effort by all the medicinemen of every pueblo was what was needed. But this had been an impossibility so far, because of a lack of cooperation among all the far-scattered pueblos. This was mainly due to the differences in language as well as some puny dissensions, even among pueblos which spoke related dialects. What they needed was an unusually smart personality, a genius no less—and all of a sudden he made his existence known, not from among their much disunited brotherhood, but in the person of a mysterious being who was sending out the most encouraging messages from a secret *estufa* at the isolated northernmost Tiwa pueblo of Taos. The *caciques* of the various other pueblos who were consulting with him described him to their people as a giant black personage with big yellow eyes, and who claimed that he was the Representative (the one taking the place) of Pohe-yemo, the Keeper of the Sun. Hence, in their estimation, he had been sent by those "Ancient Ones" in pueblo lore who had instructed their first ancestors when they emerged from the earth's womb.

The Spaniards, on the other hand, had different opinions when they first heard of him.

3. The Representative of Pohe-yemo

After the friars and several colonists had been killed at Taos and Picurís, and also at the Tewa pueblos just north of Santa Fe, and just before the capital's siege began, two young messengers from the nearby pueblo of Tesuque were apprehended while on their way to notify the pueblos of Galisteo and San Marcos south of the Villa. Although severely questioned, and even threatened, by Governor Otermín's aides, the two lads kept on insisting in telling all that they knew. They kept repeating that the Representative of Pohe-yemo, a giant black being with very big yellow eyes, had ordered the rebellion through his own representative, named Popé, the *cacique* of San Juan Pueblo, (Popé had already killed his own son-in-law for being the pueblo's governor, a Spanish institution as mentioned before.) As for the real identity of that mysterious being, all that they knew came from what their own *caciques* had told their own people, obviously instructed by Popé who had assumed the leadership of all the Tewa pueblos of which Tesuque was one.

Some of the Spanish interrogators still felt that the messengers were making up a fantastic story, while others were just as certain that it had to be the Devil himself. For had not the padres claimed that he was behind their idolatry? As for all the pueblo religious leaders who had been consulting with this superior being, they had been thoroughly captivated by his wondrous plan whereby all the Spaniards and the friars would be gotten rid of at one fell swoop.

We, of course, presuppose that Pohe-yemo's Representative had to be a real human being, and a genius at that. But who was he? Some years before, a Santa

Fe friar had commented that some of the *mestizos* and *mulatos* of Analco had been abandoning their former Christian upbringing and adopting the pagan beliefs of the nearby pueblos. From descriptive lists we know that there were *mulato* families named Naranjo in Analco at the time, and who were to flee with the Spaniards of Santa Fe in 1680 when the siege of the Villa was broken temporarily. Then, from a later irrefutable source we learn that the coordinator of the Pueblo Revolt had been a coal-black fellow (*un negro atesado*) named Domingo Naranjo. He had a black-complexioned son named Lucas Naranjo living in Santa Clara Pueblo, and another one named José Naranjo who had a much lighter complexion (probably born of a fair-skinned *mestiza* of Analco). All of them could speak Spanish well, while the father also knew how to write. These are the incontrovertible facts.

As for Domingo Naranjo's origin, he seems to have been the son of a very intelligent *mulato* who had come as a squire or manservant to a Spanish officer in the Oñate contingent of 1598, which had also brought several Tlascaltec servants of superior quality. One of these he could have married or else lived with. Later he had attached himself to another officer surnamed López Naranjo, whose name he assumed and whose livestock he herded near Santa Clara Pueblo. A result of this union was Domingo Naranjo, who in his turn had two sons named Lucas and José, the latter years later using the full name López Naranjo. All this, of course, is mere speculation or theory. But that the Pueblo Revolt of 1680 had been planned and carried out by a coal-black fellow named Domingo Naranjo, and who had two sons named Lucas and José, both of whom play their part in later events, rests on solid documentary evidence.

Now, this Domingo Naranjo had to be a strapping big man with the strong color of his African ancestry and the yellow eyes of whatever Caucasian admixture he had, which helped him convince the more spare-framed pueblo *caciques* with their brown skin and squinting dark eyes of his supernal nature. He had to be well up in years by this time, another qualification which the Indians revered as a necessary trait for wisdom. Having acquired a good knowledge of pueblo lore, he backed it up with that of his partly Tlascaltec heritage, as is evident from names of Aztec mythology which he also used. As for his inner sincerity, one can see the burning hate he had for the white European and his stern religion which had done so many injustices to all of his mixed African and Indian forebears in the past.

Hence he had unobtrusively absconded himself many years before at the pueblo of Taos, for lying furthest from prying Spanish eyes, and there he gradually convinced its leaders that he had supernatural powers—and not without the help of some feats of legerdemain, perhaps. Genius that he was, he also knew the psychology of the Spaniards with their own set of superstitions as he saw them; should they get some knowledge of his assumed being, they would conclude that it was the Devil himself, which they did. He knew well that during the week when the tenth of August fell, they would be occupied in celebrating with Masses and merriment the feast of San Lorenzo—St. Lawrence the Deacon, who was greatly revered by the Spaniards as the first of their race to have suffered martyrdom in Rome for his Christian Faith.

Naranjo could also write, as we learn from written messages which he sent to a couple of *coyote* leaders who were also literate, while the rest of them he notified about the day of vengeance in Indian fashion, by means of knots tied on deerhide thongs and cords of yucca fiber.

* * *

Many years ago, from that clear evidence I discovered, I had a duly annotated study published in *The New Mexico Historical Review*, an organ of the University of New Mexico. In it I identified Domingo Naranjo as the genius behind it all, and which knowledgeable scholars accepted. When the year 1980 was in the offing, it occurred to me that a Tertio-Centennial of the 1680 Pueblo Revolt should be celebrated as a most important event in New Mexico's history, and featuring all of our New Mexico Pueblos as its main celebrants. But soon some recently arrived, self-constituted "Indian-lovers," whose own ancestors long ago practically did away with the Native Americans back east, began reporting in the newspapers, and in pamphlets they distributed, that my identification of Black Naranjo as the Representative of Pohe-yemo was only a theory of mine, and that I was a racist besides! None of them bothered to check the sources I had used, or that I, in my long fatherly and brotherly acquaintanceship with the Rio Grande Keres pueblos, had a deeper reason for loving our Indians than they had.

Most unfortunately, such a grand celebration never came to pass, although grants had been made for this purpose, except for a modest one at San Juan Pueblo, old Popé's home. The several other pueblos had again failed to unite, and I, become a bit sarcastic for the nonce, had to tell some history confreres that once again another Domingo Naranjo had been needed to bring it all about.

(Of additional interest, the Representative of Pohe-yemo left many descendants among the Indian Naranjos of Santa Clara through his son Lucas, and among the Hispanic Naranjos nearby through his more famous son José López Naranjo—and this made me suspect with some impish glee that I myself might belong to the latter. For the maternal grandmother of my grandfather Eugenio Chávez, María Rita Torres by name, came from Río Arriba Torres folks having marital connections with their Naranjo neighbors. What I finally ascertained is that María Rita's great-granduncle, Salvador de Torres, was the one who had married Catarina Naranjo, a granddaughter of José López Naranjo, and therefore a great-granddaughter of the Representative of Pohe-yemo. To put it briefly by way of a miserable pun, I had missed being a descendant of his by an heir!)

4. Loss at El Paso del Norte

Now back to the Chaves and other refugees at El Paso del Norte in 1680-1681, and to their elderly leader Don Pedro Durán y Chaves II. Those other refugees still kept on accusing him of taking an undue share of the rations sent up by the Viceroy. And he himself was still complaining in 1681 about his own poverty, while the others said that he was profiteering in livestock and textiles. Meanwhile, he kept on plotting to impede a return of the colonists to their homeland, and finally, in 1684, his large family and that of Tomé Domínguez de Mendoza got official permission to move down to New Spain. Others of the same related bunch followed before the decade was over. They are the ancestors of prominent Chaves, Domínguez, Romero, and other people in what is now northern Mexico.

From these same sources and others, we learn about other such Chaves individuals included in Don Pedro's large group, but whose exact relationship to him cannot be ascertained for lack of evidence. There were three younger males listed respectively as Don José, Don Juan, and Don Tomás Durán y Chaves, in addition to their physical description. But, since they all abandoned the colony with him and the Domínguez de Mendozas, they merit no individual treatment here.

One sole exception is another *Don Fernando Durán y Chaves*, who was designated as the *sargento mayor* as distinct from the *capitán* bearing the same name, and who deserves treatment not only because he had very good reasons to join the others, but also because he left his mark on New Mexico. He had been stationed far north in Taos with his family when the Indians struck on that fateful August

10 of 1680.

His entire family was wiped out by the Taos rebels, except for a young son, Cristóbal, who was with him trading with the northern Utes when the massacre occurred. With them was a Sebastián de Herrera Corrales, an Andalusian whose wife and two in-laws had come to Taos with him on a visit, and who were also killed with their Chaves hosts.

All three men managed to sneak past the Taos warriors, and then the Tano and Tewa ones besieging the Villa of Santa Fe, and they finally caught up with the Río Abajo refugees. From his son's name we might hazard the guess that this Don Fernando could have been the son of Don Cristóbal and his wife Juana Domínguez de Mendoza, since he had named his own son "Cristóbal." In 1681 this Don Fernando was described as being thirty-four years old, tall and thin, of good features and wearing a thick black beard. His young son Cristóbal was sixteen or seventeen, single, tall and swarthy, with a mole on the right cheek. Both of them then fled to Mexico City to plead with the Viceroy in behalf of their immediate relatives, but returned temporarily to El Paso del Norte.

This Taos Don Fernando also had a sister, Maria de Chaves, mentioned as the wife of a Bernabé Márquez who was siding with his brother-in-law. This fellow and a Diego Márquez were half-brothers of the *coyote* Alonso Catiti, the rebel leader of the Santo Domingo Indians—evidently the result of either the rape or seduction by their father of his Indian mother. Hence Catiti had his own private reason to hate the Spaniards. (Here it must be pointed out that Popé of San Juan was not the main and only agent of Pohe-yemo's Representative—as both the Tewas and the Spaniards of Santa Fe thought, and as many still do—from that one incident when the Tesuque young messengers were questioned. While he was the leader of the Tewas north of Santa Fe, each of the other pueblos had their very own able *cacique* who, like Popé and this Alonso Catiti, had been directly summoned to war by Domingo Naranjo.)

Don Fernando's wife, slain at Taos with her guests, was not an Elena Ruíz Cáceres as I once supposed, for this woman and her husband Miguel Luján escaped the 1680 massacre with two daughters of theirs. One of these, called María, named them as her parents when she married Sebastián Martín Serrano in 1691; but in her last will and testament decades later, in 1765, she declared that this Don Fernando D. y Chaves and the same Elena Ruíz Cáceres had been her "legitimate" parents—what looks like a vain boast. Hence we do not know who Don Fernando's massacred wife was, while vaguely suspecting a past case of adultery on his part. In any case, Don Fernando and his son Cristóbal never came back to New Mexico, and one cannot blame them at all since they most sorrowfully knew that their entire family had been wiped out. *Yet the father's name perdured in the valley of Taos as the "Río de Don Fernando" (from which the town of Don Fernando de Taos got its name when founded some hundred and ten years later), and in the lands which "Don Fernando de Chaves" owned prior to 1680 at present Ranchos de Taos.*

* * *

As for the female Chaves side, those who were not named were among the minor children, or else the wives of other refugees with different appellations. Of these latter there were two unnamed daughters of old Don Pedro, the wives, as we learn elsewhere, of an Antonio de Carvajal and Pedro Márquez. One exception was that sister of Don Fernando of Taos, Maria de Chaves, married to Bernabé Márquez as just said; another one was Isabel de Chaves who added "*de Bohórques*" to her name, and was the wife of Juan Domínguez de Mendoza. As shown before, she was the sister of Don Pedro Duran y Chaves II who had also married into her husband's family.

There was another *María de Chaves*, perhaps older than the other María previously named, and who eventually returned home to New Mexico. Her husband, the *sargento mayor* Francisco de Tapia, had died before the Pueblo Revolt, and she was living in dire need with her children at Corpus Christi de Ysleta when her daughter Luisa de Tapia married an Antonio Ramírez in 1685. Of particular interest because of its historical association was the wedding on December 23, 1693, of another daughter, María de Tapia, to a newly-arrived soldier named Miguel Gutiérrez from San Luis Potosí, and designated as an *español*. For it took place in Santa Fe just a week after Governor Vargas took the Villa by force from the Tano Indians. Later, also in Santa Fe in 1698, her son Francisco de Tapia got married to a Magdalena Nieto.

But how this faithful Tapia widow was related to any of the Chaves folk previously treated, there is no way of telling so far. Because she came back to New Mexico, she might have been more closely related to the one and only Chaves family man who did come back. This was *Don Fernando Durán y Chaves*, the *capitán*, who returned to his inheritance of primogeniture, to the Chaves *estancia* of El

Tunque, or what was left of it. However, because she took up residence in Santa Fe where her Tapia in-laws lived, María de Chaves and her Tapia children find no mention in connection with the *capitán* Don Fernando Durán y Chaves at his place in the Rio Abajo—the second one of this full name in the line of primogeniture whose life and many adventures begin the Second Part of this narrative as the Second Progenitor of the New Mexico Chaves clan.

PART TWO
The Second Progenitor

The Vargas Reconquest of 1693, by José Cisneros.

Don Fernando Durán y Chaves II

Doña Lucía Hurtado de Salas

1. Like Father Like Son

When the 1680 Pueblo Revolt broke out, he was a *capitán* living in the ancestral *estancia* of El Tunque, or what was left of it, with his wife *Lucía Hurtado de Salas y Trujillo* and their four little children, besides a couple of servants. This inherited homestead, as mentioned before, stood somewhere in the area of the present Ranchos de Santa Ana now owned by the Santa Ana Indians, whose pueblo lies directly to the west across the Rio Grande. The four small children's names were *Bernardo, Pedro, Antonio,* and *Isabel.* During past decades other people had moved in closer by, as remarked previously, evidently through a grant made by the infamous Governor Peñalosa. For the grantee was a certain Anaya married to a Domínguez de Mendoza woman, both of whom will be met soon under the most terrible circumstances. The spot where they and two other related families lived was being called Angostura, a "narrowness" in the valley caused by a barren spur coming down from the eastern San Pedro mountain area, now called the Ortiz range.

Perhaps to distinguish this Angostura from his own place of residence just south of it, Don Fernando began calling the latter "Bernalillo" (Old Spanish for "Little Bernie") after his eldest child for whom he must have harbored a special affection. From what one gathers in the contemporary accounts, his place now stood on the western bank of the Rio Grande—the latter having changed its course somewhere below Angostura to flow down the middle of the widening valley instead of along its western edge, as it does now. Angostura with its fertile lands (present Algodones) had been left on the eastern bank up to San Felipe Pueblo, which at that time stood, as previously, just north of the Tunque arroyo before it reached the river. All this has to be kept in mind in order to understand what was to take place on that fateful August of 1680.

Now to this Don Fernando's own identity and his place in the line of descent. Ever since first treating about the matter many years ago, I always presumed that he was the firstborn son of the first Don Fernando and his Carvajal wife. This was principally because he inherited the ancestral Tunque grant, and also because he was the only Chaves who insisted on returning home with his family, whereas the rest of his many Chaves relatives had chosen to abandon their homeland forever. But gradually I began having my doubts, chiefly because of his age of about thirty in 1681 (and "forty" in the same year), and then in later testimonies of 1691 when he gave his age as forty-four, and sixty in a subsequent one of 1711. On the average, these would place his birth around the year 1650. Now, as we have already seen, the elder Don Fernando had one known son, Cristóbal, who was twenty-four in that right-of-sanctuary incident with his uncle Pedro back in 1663; hence this our Don Fernando was some eleven years younger. Granting whatever inaccuracies were recorded as to ages, he most certainly was not the first-born son of the family.

But then we have a testimony which he later gave at El Paso del Norte, that he himself remembered the execution of eight men far back in 1643—perhaps as a little boy, when that affair was still fresh among the people. Later on he must have witnessed his elder brother Cristobal's estrangement from their father by siding with their uncle Pedro and the Dominguez de Mendozas. Moreover, we have good Padre Bernal again, who in 1669 had mourned the death of the first Don Fernando. In a similar letter to the Inquisition of the following year, 1770, he praised this our younger Don Fernando, who was an *alférez* at the time, as "a youth of good repute." Like father like son, we might say again. It is sometime after this that he could have married his Lucía Hurtado de Salas, when we consider the four small children they had by 1680. It also speaks well of him that just three years before, in 1677, the latest new governor, an upright man named Don Antonio de Otermín, had made the young man a member of the "*Cabildo* of the Kingdom."

As to why this much younger Fernando had inherited the old Chaves patrimony instead of his much older brother Cristóbal, we know that the latter was already dead or gone by 1680, or well before. And even before this he seems to have become alienated from his father when he married a woman of the impious Domínguez de Mendoza people and, like his uncle Pedro, adopted their impieties among other unsavory habits. Whatever, here we have our second Don Fernando Durán y Chaves who likewise despised the Domínguez de Mendozas and his several Chaves relatives allied with them, and ever so anxious to return to his dear inheritance with his growing family, which he eventually did.

2. The Pueblo Revolt Again

This brings us back to the Pueblo Revolt of 1680, specifically in connection with our Don Fernando and his entire family. From here on, too, we fortunately have many details about him in that year, and in the ones which followed until his death many years later. On that fateful August 10th, the friars of San Felipe and Cochiti had joined their confrere at Santo Domingo, which lay between the other two pueblos, in order to celebrate the favorite Spanish feast of San Lorenzo. There the three padres, along with four soldiers and the wife of one of them, were massacred by the Santo Domingo Indians. These same warriors then went downstream along the Rio Grande as far as San Felipe Pueblo where its people had so far not joined in the rebellion.

Living close to it were three members of a certain Naranjo family, probably descendants of that *mulato* from Analco among the original servants of the first Don Pedro who had married a San Felipe woman, as well as somehow related to Domingo Naranjo up in Taos. The Santo Domingo warriors killed an older individual named Bartolomé Naranjo for refusing to join them, while two younger brothers of his managed to escape. These two youngsters, named Juan Lorenzo and Francisco Lorenzo Naranjo, we shall meet later on, and in the company of a certain José or Josepe (also a Naranjo) during a brief Spanish military entry in the following year. For the latter turned out to be one of the two sons of that noted Domingo Naranjo.

From here the same warriors proceeded down to nearby Angostura and killed three families living there. The first consisted of a lone woman and her little girl—the husband, a fellow named Cuellar, being away at the time. Of more interest to us was the sad fate of Agustín de Carvajal, that close friend and brother-in-law of the first Don Fernando de Chaves. By now sixty or more years old, he seems to have always had bad luck, matrimonially and otherwise, while living in the perilous Galisteo district near the Comanche plains; finally he had moved to Angostura in his old age with a third wife, an old widow named Damiana Domínguez de Mendoza, obviously invited to live there by the grantee Cristóbal de Anaya who was his brother-in-law; both of them were now married to a couple of sisters of that gifted scoundrel Tomé Domínguez de Mendoza. The rebels killed Carvajal, his wife, a grown daughter by a previous marriage, and another woman.

But of much greater significance was the massacre of this Anaya and his family. Cristóbal was the eldest son of Francisco Anaya de Almazán, an early colonist born in Mexico City of prominent and most religious parents from Salamanca in Spain. However, this his eldest son had turned out differently, whether before or after he married Leonor Domínguez de Mendoza. He had become a religious scoffer, and as a result was summoned down to Mexico City for trial by the Inquisition; this, it was said, had caused his father's death. After undergoing some sort of ceremonial penance down there, he had returned a worse scoffer than before. So it looks as though Governor Peñalosa, to spite the first Don Fernando de Chaves at Tomé's suggestion, had given him this grant in Angostura. To make matters short, the Santo Domingo Indians killed Anaya, his wife, six children, and four other persons staying with him, leaving their naked bodies piled across the threshold.

This is when Don Fernando Durán y Chaves, just a short distance south at his Bernalillo, barely escaped with his young family. The only reason for this was the previous change in the river's course mentioned before. It was also in flood at this late date, a fact referred to several times in the accounts, even as far down as El Paso del Norte; hence the winter before must have been an extraordinarily long and snowy one. Had our Don Fernando gotten an inkling as to what was happening in Angostura further up across the river? If so, he had quickly packed some horses with his family and whatever provisions they could carry, and then fled southward to join the people of the neighboring homesteads on his side of the river, and all the way down to those of his wife's relatives in the vicinity of what is now present Albuquerque.

What we do know is that on the previous day, August 9, the *teniente* Alonso García for the Río Abajo at the time, had left his own *estancia* of San Antonio south of Sandía on the eastern bank with four soldiers, for the purpose of investigating rumors of previous unrest at the far western pueblos of Jémez. At Zia Pueblo closer by they ran into the fleeing *alcalde* of the Jémez pueblos with four soldiers and a friar, all of whom told him that the Jémez had already killed another friar stationed among them. Then here at Zia they all managed to rescue the local padre and three Spanish fellows who had taken refuge inside the mission church. This done, they all went back to Sandía which was still at peace. On the following day García went back to investigate the pueblo of San Felipe, and so learned that its warriors were also on the warpath by the time he got there.

This is when he might have alerted Don Fernando in the nick of time, and then conducted him with his family to the *estancias* further south.

However, during the night of the 10th, the small pueblo of Puaray and the very large one of Sandía pounced upon all the Spaniards living on their own eastern side of the river, killing practically all of them. García figured that by now 120 Río Abajo colonists had been slain. By the 14th he had assembled 1500 others at the pueblo of Isleta further south along with seven of the surviving Mission padres. For the the Isleta Indians had not rebelled so far. This Isleta *Alcaldía* itself had seven Spanish *estancias*, most of them belonging to other Chaves heads of families and to the Domínguez de Mendozas. Here on the same day, García called a *junta* of all the family heads, when it was resolved that, since the lord governor and the northern colonists were all dead, and these of the south were short of munitions, it was best to keep on fleeing further south until they met an armed party from New Mexico which had previously been sent to El Paso del Norte, there to meet an expected Mission supply train from Mexico City. All signed in the affirmative, including Don Fernando Durán y Chaves.

Six days later, on August 20, they were overtaken by three fellows from faraway northern Taos who had escaped the massacre there. One of them was that *sargento mayor* Don Fernando de Chaves of Taos, and the other that Sebastián de Herrera who had escaped with him. (Here the chronicler overlooked Fernando's young son Cristóbal, who had escaped with them and later passed muster at El Paso del Norte.) These three first brought the startling news that Governor Otermín and his Santa Fe people were still alive, though sorely besieged. Hence a second meeting was called upon reaching the southernmost *Alcaldía* of Senecú on August 24th. Here everyone, including the Taos escapees and the local inhabitants, voted to keep on fleeing south. For their numbers had now been increased by the settlers living here and the well-christianized Piro Indians of the Senecú and Socorro pueblos.

Yet there was one single dissenter, but he was overruled by all of his peers. "*The capitán Don Fernando Durán y Chaves said that it was his opinion that, leaving the small camp safeguarded, it would be well to go back to the Villa of Santa Fe to learn for certain whether they are alive or dead.*" This lone contrary opinion he duly signed. Among the rest who most emphatically did not want to go back to Santa Fe were his uncle Don Pedro and the Domínguez de Mendoza brothers.

3. To El Paso del Norte

In the meantime, Governor Otermín and his Santa Fe people were also on their way downriver, after having broken the siege long enough to give them time to escape. At San Felipe Pueblo, vacated for the nonce, they could see its Indians taunting them from atop the mesa across the river, and at Angostura they buried the naked corpses which they found there. On August 26 they passed through Sandía Pueblo which also lay abandoned at the time, as were, of course, the homesteads of Alonso García and Doña Luisa de Montoya, or Trujillo. (The latter place still bore the name of the grandmother of Don Fernando's wife, and whom we shall meet when we come to the latter's ancestry.) Finally, on September 13, they caught up with the Río Abajo refugees at a far southern spot called Fray Cristóbal, where the latter had been awaiting their arrival. This was because Governor Otermín had sent a message ahead to Alonso García, who must have been immensely surprised by it, to say the least, as were the other heads of families.

We wonder if our Don Fernando gloated over the news by reminding the rest of his previous lone opinion, and which they had summarily rejected, of going back to Santa Fe to ascertain the fate of its people. Very likely he kept his peace to avoid further dissensions. Regarding the place just mentioned, Fray Cristóbal was an already famous historic spot across the Rio Grande well below Socorro, and where the old *Camino Real* entered the desert route of La Jornada del Muerto (the Dead Man's Route and not the Journey of Death as often mistranslated).

By September 18 the now combined large parties of refugees reached a spot called La Salineta, again only a place-name on the Royal Highway, which was regal only in name, some twelve miles north of El Paso del Norte. The valley here was flooded by the swollen Rio Grande, this again attributed by the chronicler to the extraordinary amount of melting snows on the high northern sierras. Here, on September 29, a roster was taken up of the heads of families, when Don Fernando passed muster "with eight lean and sore-backed horses, an harquebus, and a sword; he is married, with four small children and two servants; he was robbed by the enemy; and he signed it." Here his uncle Don Pedro de Chaves and all the Domínguez de Mendozas registered many more possessions by far, for having had more time, and a large amount of servant help, to gather all they could before leaving their homesteads.

Upon reaching the Guadalupe Mission of El Paso del Norte in the first week of October, Governor Otermín set up his royal camp at a place known as La Toma (The Taking). It was the very spot where Don Juan de Oñate had "taken" formal possession of New Mexico far back in 1598. This he renamed El Real de San Lorenzo in honor of the saint on whose feast the Pueblo Revolt had started; the chapel built there was named after the Virgin Mary in her New Mexican title of La Conquistadora. In the same month two other villages were founded, called San Pedro de Alcántara and El Santísimo Sacramento. From here on through the remaining weeks of 1680, and throughout the years 1681 and 1682, there occurred all those quarrelsome incidents previously treated in the section concerning Don Pedro Durán y Chaves and his Domínguez de Mendoza in-laws.

In April of the following year, 1681, Governor Otermín called a *junta de guerra* at El Paso del Norte. Since several of the poorer folks had been slipping away toward Sonora and Parral far down south, while the more affluent ones like the Chaves and Domínguez were ever clamoring for a more official approval due to their status, he wanted to know which families favored an eventual return to their New Mexico homeland. Don Fernando signed up among those willing to go back: "Considering first of all the service of God, it is well for us to enter the Kingdom of New Mexico, if we have stores of munitions, and everything necessary." The clerk then added: "Of the two evils of hunger and war, he regards hunger as more calamitous." This sounds like a note of sarcasm, or else he was agreeing that settlers, like soldiers, do best with food in their bellies.

Here it must be mentioned that a big shipment of arms and other provisions had previously arrived from Mexico City for those who wanted to resettle New Mexico, hence a suit of armor which he later declared as part of his readiness. Now as a prospective re-settler, he signed a second declaration at El Paso: "The *capitán* Don Fernando Durán y Chaves, *vecino*,[1] who declared that he had received the equivalent of two hundred and fifty pesos in silver which his Majesty gave him, in the form of clothing in the same quantity as the rest, along with a plow, an axe, and four hoes. He is married, and has as distinguishing marks a good stature and fair complexion. He is a native of New Mexico and is about thirty years old."

1. "Neighbor" literally, but meaning settler or inhabitant as distinct from the native Pueblo Indians, a term still used until recent times.

4. A Futile Expedition

This brings us to an armed expedition which Governor Otermín made into New Mexico in the latter months of 1681. His purpose was to find out if a return of the settlers was both possible and safe, and as a member of his staff he appointed our young Don Fernando. The other leaders had to sign up for it, including the Domínguez de Mendozas, and who did so with their characteristic reservations. In his turn, the governor placed Tomé Domínguez in charge of the combat units, and later chose his brother Juan to lead the actual reconnoitering force. On September 8 at San Lorenzo de la Toma, Don Fernando averred "that he was willing to assist in the service of both Majesties, declaring that he was married, and that the arms he has for the service of both Majesties are a sword, harquebus, leather jacket, suit of armor, leather shield, and eight horses; he declared that he is forty years old, and he signed it." (His age had increased by ten years, patently the clerk's error.)

Then, between November 7 and 10, at El Ancón de Fray García on the way north (present Rincón near Hatch), he was listed again as having passed muster "with eight tame horses and all personal arms except a suit of armor, and a servant boy." Evidently he was not wearing the suit of armor at the time. Also to be noticed so far, Don Fernando, unlike the rest, often made references to God in his declarations. It is like an echo of the expressed sentiments of the first Don Fernando Durán y Chaves. Yet he was prone to make a pessimistic remark which stands out like an aphorism. For it was around this time, when recalling that beheading of eight men far back in 1643, that he referred to his New Mexico as a "miserable kingdom." He did not mean the land itself, of course, but the excesses of several bad governors and their henchmen which had made life miserable for everyone. Curiously, a son of his would be using the very same expression forty years later, as if he had often heard it from his father's lips.

Having at last reached Isleta Pueblo by December, the Spanish force entered the Indian village after a minor resistance by the natives. The greater number of them appeared friendly, but, as they told the governor, they were fearful of the northern pueblos and the Apaches roving nearby who would wreak their vengeance upon them after the Spaniards left, or should they be defeated. On the 7th and 8th of December, the friars with the expedition received the inhabitants back into the Church with great ceremony. However, from here on the expedition turned out to be a total failure.

When the reconnoitering force was sent up north under Juan Domínguez de Mendoza, Otermín's firm instructions were that the Indians which they encountered had to be treated with every kindness, and with promises of being completely forgiven as had those of Isleta. But soon Domínguez and his men discovered that all the Tiwas of Puaray, Sandía, and Alameda had fled into the mountains; hence at each abandoned pueblo he and his soldiers looted all of the many provisions which these people had left behind when they fled. At Alameda on the river's west bank they found one very old woman whom the natives had purposely left behind; she spoke good Spanish and gave them much information, but the reason she is brought in here is because she said that as a girl she had been the handmaid of Doña Isabel Holguín—that mother-in-law of the first Don Fernando Durán y Chaves.

Further north they found the Keres of San Felipe, Santo Domingo, and Cochiti, as well as the Jémez, all ensconced atop the high mesas above Cochiti; in fact, they had just been joined by the Tiwas whom the forces had first hoped to pacify further south. All that these soldiers encountered here were a couple of peaceful sallies by some of the Indians which soon proved to be no more than tricks of theirs. There were also insults flung down from the mesas, as when the *coyotes* among them called the Spaniards *cornudos cabrones y llorones*, [2] and as a result several skirmishes followed. In-between such skirmishes, and the tricks being played by the Indians on their perches, a couple of Spanish-speaking youths had sneaked down to warn the Spaniards of their treachery. One was that young Francisco Lorenzo Naranjo of San Felipe who with his brother had escaped being massacred the year before. The other was a fellow calling himself Josepe (old form of José) who had once been a servant of Sebastián de Herrera. And here, by pure coincidence, the latter was one of the Spaniards present, along with his old friend of Taos, the *sargento mayor* Don Fernandez de Chaves. Now Josepe told them he had fled to El Paso del Norte the previous year (with the faithful Naranjos of Santa Fe's Analco), but soon thereafter had come back to the New Mexico pueblos. Now he wanted to rejoin the Spaniards along with Francisco Lorenzo Naranjo.

A week later, at Governor Otermín's camp in Isleta, Josepe was seen in the

2. Cuckolds, pimps, and cry-babies.

company of a Diego Naranjo, eighty years old, who claimed to be from San Felipe Pueblo and had come down to render helpful service to the governor. The Spaniards recognized him as an *hechicero*, but it is Josepe who revealed him to be a spy for the rebels. (Was this warlock the grandfather of the San Felipe Naranjos, and closely related to that Domingo Naranjo of Taos, the Representative of Pohe-yemo?) As for young Josepe, evidently the latter's lighter-complexioned son, he was now siding with the Spaniards once more, later to be know by the full name he gave of López Naranjo. This supposition will continue gathering more strength, while the Spaniards at that time were still ignorant, and for years to come would continue to be so, of the real identity of that mysterious being who had successfully planned and carried out the revolt of the previous year.

To make matters short, Juan Domínguez de Mendoza and his force came back, greatly frustrated, to Otermín's headquarters at Isleta Pueblo where our Don Fernando was waiting with him for the results of their mission. The governor in his turn soundly blamed them all for the expedition's failure, pointing to their senseless tactics as well as their looting of the vacated pueblos. Besides, what was troubling him the most at this very time was the discovery of more spies among the Isletas, as well as the unseen presence of Apache warriors in the vicinity. Hence he called another *junta* on December 23 and 24, to get an opinion from his staff and the other leaders as to whether or not to continue what was supposed to have been a peaceful invasion. Don Fernando and his kinsman, Ignacio Baca, voted to cease disturbing the Indians and have the expedition return to El Paso del Norte.

To quote the notary in full, "Don Fernando de Chaves feels in conscience that, attending the service of God, it will be a very good thing for the royal army to leave immediately without delay to the *plaza de armas* of San Lorenzo, withdrawing from the severe climate of these parts. For the horses are in such a state that they will perish in a month, because there are now very few *bestias*[3] that can be saddled and most of the soldiers have to stand watch on foot. It is now impossible to punish the enemy because they are united and assembled in the roughest part of the sierra, and the feigned peace that they made was for the purpose of killing us treacherously, as has been learned and is well known; furthermore we

3. Not "beasts" as sometimes translated, but "steeds," an expression still current in New Mexico.

are now besieged by spies; and the principal argument is that there are no horses."

And so Governor Otermín produced an *auto* under date of December 31, stating his reasoned resolve to return to El Paso del Norte, while also bringing along a fair number of the Isleta Indians who volunteered to leave their ancient homeland and share their future with the *cristianos,* as had the Piros of Socorro the year before. (These new allies were settled at the village of El Santísimo Sacramento which subsequently was called Corpus Christi de Ysleta.)

After this, life at El Paso del Norte and its newly founded New Mexico villages continued peacefully enough, except for the usual squabbling common to any community, or an occasional minor raid by some roving Indians of that area. There had to be considerable if silent unrest among the faithful colonists, and this all due to the fact that the El Paso region had precious little land for farming and, worse still, very poor of the same for grazing. A return home to their New Mexico was the only solution. The real noise came from the Domínguez de Mendozas and Don Pedro de Chaves with their inter-related families. Those of Tomé and Don Pedro managed to get permission to leave for New Spain in 1684, following the arrival of a new governor, Don Domingo Petríz de Cruzate, while the rest did the same in the years following.

This new governor had made our Don Fernando one of the two regents of the El Paso military post, and in the following year, 1685, he forbade both of them from absenting themselves lest the post and colony were left unprotected. Apparently this is why he took no part in an armed entry which Cruzate made into New Mexico in this same year. This also spared him the sorrow of witnessing certain cruelties perpetrated on the pueblos by this expedition.

* * *

What we hear next about Don Fernando Durán y Chaves comes from three matrimonial investigations of 1689, 1691, and 1693, all of which brings us into a new period in his life. The reconquest of his New Mexico by the famed Don Diego de Vargas was approaching. In the first one of 1689 he gave his age as forty-four when testifying for a Madrid-Arbizu wedding, and when the notary referred to him as "a former *capitán* of the Kingdom." Obviously he meant by this that Don Fernando had held this title even before the Pueblo Revolt of 1680. In the next one, two years later when testifying for a Martín-Luján couple, he still was forty-four and gave El Paso del Norte as his place of residence; he and his wife Doña Lucía Hurtado witnessed the marriage on September 24. The third one of 1693 concerned the wedding of an Apodaca-Durán pair, for whom he and his friend Antonio Jorge (to be met again) acted as witnesses.

This last wedding is of particular interest because the bride's previous husband had been killed in a battle of Zia in New Mexico five years previously, and had been buried in the ruined house of Juan Domínguez de Mendoza; then, eight months ago, his bones had been brought back to El Paso del Norte and reburied in its church. This second burial refers to a memorable peaceful entry into New Mexico by the current governor, Don Diego de Vargas, in September of the preceding year, 1692. The wedding itself, on June 30, 1693, took place just six months prior to this governor's return of the colonists to Santa Fe in this same year.

By this time Don Fernando had engendered six more children in addition to the four little ones he had brought from his New Mexico home back in 1680. Their names according to their ages were *Francisco, Luís, Nicolás, María, Catarina*—and last, as commented at length long before—a second Pedro whom his father named *Pedro Gómez.* (There was also an eleventh one who was not with the family, and about whom Don Fernando must have felt embarrassed; her name was *Clara,* his bastard daughter by some *mestiza* of El Paso del Norte, and whom we shall meet again, if briefly and if by chance.) At any rate, both Don Fernando and his faithful Doña Lucía were hopefully looking forward to a return to their ancestral home, confident in the promises which Don Diego de Vargas was making around this time.

5. The Vargas Reconquest, 1692-1693

Don Diego de Vargas Zapata Luján Ponce de León, Marqués de la Nava de Barcinas (always being misquoted and misspelled as "de las Brazinas") stands out in New Mexico's colonial history as the great Reconquistador that he was, along with his great lengthy name and noble title. A scion of the ancient noble Vargas family of Madrid, he was a most upright and very religious person, while no less a very sad and disappointed one. For, as recent discoveries of his letters reveal, he had left Spain for the New World to make a fortune, and this for the single purpose of saving his old ancestral properties which had fallen into debt. While waiting a long while in Mexico City for such a rich assignment, and in spite of his pious sentiments, he formed an extramarital alliance with a lady of stature by whom he had two sons.

But, instead of getting some gold-rich province to rule in other parts of America as he had dreamed, he was sent to reconquer a so-called kingdom rich only in adobe and everything this term represents. At first, New Mexico's grand designation as a Kingdom must have raised his hopes high when he got the appointment, and no less his inherent piety after reading *El Mercurio Volante*, a popular publication in Mexico City which glorified the twenty-one Franciscan Martyrs of 1680 in that very same Kingdom.

Hence one of his first solemn acts after reaching El Paso del Norte, in May of 1692, was to formally bestow all the local Missions, and in particular those much older ones of the New Mexico Martyrs, to the current Franciscan *Custodio*. This his *auto* was co-signed by our Don Fernando Durán y Chaves and three other leaders. He likewise had fallen in love with the little statue of La Conquistadora in her chapel at El Real de San Lorenzo after hearing her story from the colonists. He rendered her title in his more genteel *Nuestra Señora de la Conquista* (Our Lady of the Conquest), also calling her the "Queen of the Kingdom of New Mexico and its Villa of Santa Fe" when he wrote to the Viceroy of his intention of restoring her to her former throne (the destroyed parish church which he planned to rebuild).

And heading his forces in the hands of the *Alférez Real* would go that same pendant-banner which Don Juan de Oñate had used in his own original *conquista* a century before—displaying on one face the image of Nuestra Señora de los Remedios, Patroness of the Spaniards of Mexico City since its conquest by Cortés, and on the other the quartered arms of León and Castile. It looks as though he had done some research before leaving the capital of New Spain.

Very likely impressed by our Don Fernando's ardent desire to return to his homeland, Governor Vargas had made him one of his chief aides or counselors—and was to honor him by appointing him as the *Alférez Real* of the Royal Pendant in both his *Entradas* into Santa Fe as we shall see. In a way, it was also because so many of the more prominent leaders had left the colony, following the example of the Pedro de Chaves and Domínguez de Mendoza group. For this reason Don Diego had brought along a goodly number of officers and soldiers who were originally from Spain. Moreover, he had contracted with the Viceroy to have a large number of Spanish families recruited in the Valley of Mexico and at the Mines of Zacatecas; for this purpose he had already sent two men to do all this recruiting down in those centers, but such families were not to arrive until much later, in the summers of 1694 and 1695.

It is with these new Spain-born soldiers, added to the number of the old colonists bearing arms, that he mounted an expedition to reconnoiter New Mexico in the fall of 1692. During this sally all of his men were amazed by the way his personal charisma (to use a word so much abused and overworked these days) seemed to work like a charm at every Rio Grande pueblo they reached, particularly when he pointed to the Remedios pennant as the sign and promise of brotherly love which was to exist among their people and the Spaniards alike. More as a matter of fact, the Indian pueblos had become disunited once more during the past decade. Old Black Naranjo was dead and gone by now. While those of the remaining old *caciques* and their younger assistants kept their thoughts to themselves for the nonce, the ordinary inhabitants at large seemed relieved, for they were at base a peaceful people. They wanted no more fighting, either with the Spaniards or with the wild tribes which had been invading them for as long as they could remember. Or was it because they missed the former Mission supply trains which had brought many things they now sorely missed?

And so it was that on September 14, 1692, Don Diego de Vargas and his limited cohorts entered the historic plaza of Santa Fe for a formal possession of the Villa and the entire Kingdom as well. During the past decade the Tanos of the Galisteo pueblos had turned the town into an adobe fortress, in great part by using the adobes of the large parish church to wall up the street entrances. Now the occupying Tano chieftains gave Don Diego free rein, with whatever unfriendly reservations they most certainly had, to parade his panoplied troops in formation until they halted at attention in front of the gubernatorial *casas reales*. After the *Te Deum* had been chanted by the friars, *the royal Remedios standard still raised on high by the mounted Alférez Real Don Fernando Durān y Chaves and his aide Antonio Jorge,* the lord governor and the head of the padres delivered their formal addresses of brotherhood to the natives, most of whom could not understand what they said. This done, Don Diego and his troops were soon on their way back to El Paso del Norte, to begin preparations for the colonists' return in the following year.

* * *

Late in the fall of 1693, Governor Vargas and his small army of new Spanish soldiers and colonial men-at-arms—the latter with their families and whatever household goods they had for re-settling the land after thirteen years of exile—set out for what was called a second *Entrada* into their old Kingdom. Once again, on December 16, the same ceremonial of the previous year was repeated on the Santa Fe plaza. Here Don Diego himself wrote: "I, the said Governor and Captain-General, about the eleventh hour of the same day, made my entry into the Villa of Santa Fe. . . with the squadron on the march and in company of the very illustrious Cabildo of this the said Villa and Kingdom, *its high sheriff and Alférez Real, the Capitán Don Fernando Durán y Chaves, carrying the standard referred to in these acts, and under which the land was [originally] conquered.*"

Sometime after this Don Diego requested the Tanos to re-roof the old Analco chapel of San Miguel which was still standing, in order to provide a home for the statue of La Conquistadora which, he told them, was still enclosed in one of the carts—for shouldn't they do this much for such a queenly Lady? For these Indians, of course, this was so much gibberish, but they then gave the oncoming bad weather as the excuse for not doing so.

This bad weather is what they had been looking forward to, and it soon materialized in a thick snowstorm coupled with the coldest winds, as it sometimes happens to this day in late December. The governor had encamped the colonists well away from the town, at a partly sheltered spot by the northwestern hills now called Rosario. As the storm grew worse the Tanos began taunting the troops outside from their high flat rooftops, telling them that both they and their families would soon perish from the cold, while more warriors would be coming down from the north to make their destruction complete. All this, of course, was the greatest of shocks to Don Diego de Vargas, still glorying in his peaceable acts of conquest of the year before, and so he kept waiting for some miraculous solution to this totally unexpected impasse.

But his men, particularly those who feared that their wives and their children might freeze to death, kept insisting on a direct attack on the Villa in fullest force. Don Diego finally gave in to their demands, and the full attack was made in the darkness just before dawn, when the Tanos least expected it. During the fierce assault many of the Indians were killed, and after the Spaniards' victory a goodly number of their leaders were executed. Don Diego's dream of a bloodless reconquest had been completely shattered, and more blood was to be shed in the years that immediately followed.

The new colonists from New Spain which Governor Vargas had contracted for took a long time in arriving. Six months later, in June of 1694, came the *Españoles-Mexicanos*, that is, the Spanish families from the great Valley of Mexico, by now much-restored Spaniards even if one or the other family had a sire born in Spain. The second group from the Mines of Zacatecas, which arrived in July of the following year, 1695, was similarly composed, but only partially. For many of the Spanish folks recruited there had backed out, and Don Diego's agent had replaced them with people from a lower stratum; these were settled in Santa Fe's Analco, in the former homes of the *mestizos* and *mulatos* who had stayed down in El Paso del Norte. And so the reconquered kingdom started anew in about the same way that it had begun after the first conquest under Oñate.

6. *Back Home at Last*

This whole section being the story of Don Fernando Durán y Chaves the Second, and of a new start of the Chaves clan in their old homeland, we leave Santa Fe alone with her governmental and other local affairs. For, as we have seen, the Chaves were Río Abajo people, along with many other families among the returning colonists who wanted to resettle their ancestral lands as soon as possible. Governor Vargas was opposed to it for a time, and this is when Don Fernando leased some land west of the villa near the Pueblo Quemado (present Agua Fría) from a brother-in-law of his, Juan Lucero de Godoy, who was married to his wife's sister Isabel de Salazar; her adoptive mother, old Doña Bernardina de Salas y Trujillo, mentioned far back, was staying with them at the time.

But a couple of years later, sometime around 1696, Don Fernando was back at his beloved Bernalillo *estancia* with his large family and other related ones, besides others which had formerly lived still further south in the great valley of the Rio Grande. At first Governor Vargas had been loath to let anyone leave the safe environment of Santa Fe, mainly because the roving Apaches had become a most serious menace in the south. But the then great curve of the river by his own property, Don Fernando must have figured, offered sufficient protection. Hence those other families which had once lived further south also moved into his formerly vast *estancia* and its vicinity to await the day when the Apaches were driven out for good.

Other families which had lived in the great Tewa valley north of Santa Fe also went back to their ancestral homes, along with some of the friars for restoring the old missions in that area. Here the governor was to found the new Villa of Santa Cruz de la Cañada in 1695, with the new Spanish colony which had arrived from the Valley of Mexico the year before. However, a new Indian revolt broke out in this north Tewa valley in the following year. Four friars were killed at their mission posts, as well as a number of families. The revolt had been started by a black fellow living in Santa Clara pueblo, Lucas Naranjo by name. He was none other than the son of Domingo, long dead by now, the quondam Representative of Pohe-yemo! Governor Vargas quickly went up to quell the rebellion, and in his coterie was that Josepe mentioned several times before, who ever since had worked himself into this new governor's good graces. Around this time he had gone to Santa Clara to see his black brother Lucas as if for a parley, and there he killed him and cut off his head, and this he brought to Governor Vargas to further ingratiate himself. Subsequently this José López Naranjo, as he was now calling himself, would become the head of pueblo auxiliary troops in many a campaign to come.

Lucas Naranjo had also contacted the nearest southern pueblos to join his revolt. At Jémez a fifth padre was killed. Aware of this plot which had so suddenly worked its effect in the north, Governor Vargas had written to Don Fernando down in Bernalillo, where he was the *alcalde mayor* of that area which included the Keres pueblos of San Felipe, Santo Domingo and Cochiti, ordering him to bring all the Bernalillo settlers up to Santa Fe. In fact, it was Don Fernando who had forewarned the governor, and now he wrote back that his Lordship's plan was unfeasible, hence he was going to assemble his people atop the high mesa on his side of the river where the San Felipe Indians now had their pueblo. This tactic proved to be a much better one, which also kept the San Felipes from joining the revolt should it have spread down to this area.

* * *

In this connection, by way of another needed break, there are two most interesting traditions which were related to me by dear friends of mine, the old men of San Felipe and Cochiti Pueblos, almost fifty years ago. Those of both villages boasted to me that their respective people had not killed their own mission padres in that great Indian Pueblo Revolt of long ago—meaning the famous one of 1680. They had even purposely saved their lives, they said. I told them that they were partly right, since the friars of San Felipe and Cochiti, and the one of Santo Domingo, had all been slain by the Santo Domingo Indians at their own pueblo when the three padres had gathered there to celebrate the feast of San Lorenzo on the 10th of August in 1680.

But these good men insisted on the truth of their own versions as they had been passed down from their wise forefathers. Those of Cochiti maintained that their padre had been carried out to safety, wrapped in a blanket like an old woman, on the shoulders of a sturdy young man. On the other hand, those of San Felipe related how their own ancestors, when their pueblo stood atop their neighboring mesa, had seen the fleeing Cochiti padre emerging from the cottonwood groves below, and then had brought him up to safety among them; later on, when their people had run out of drinking water, he cut his wrists and thereby furnished them with plenty of it until the crisis was over.

It was some years later, when I was concentrating on New Mexico's past history, that I discovered that those wise old men were right, if quite mistaken about the correct event. This event was that of the Lucas Naranjo rebellion of 1696, when my ancestor Don Fernando Durán y Chaves had brought up his own Bernalillo people to the easily defended mesa pueblo of the San Felipe Indians. So it could very well be true that the Indians of Cochiti, upon learning what was happening up in the Santa Clara or Tewa valley, had taken their missionary out of their own pueblo as a safety precaution, and disguised as a helpless old woman. And so it is just as likely that he had reached San Felipe to find a safe refuge there, and among Don Fernando's Spanish colonists as well.

As for the miraculous fountains from his cut wrists, this must have later evolved from some padre's sermon far back, when he told the story of Moses striking water out of a rock in the arid desert of Sinai. This same San Felipe tale, I also learned later, was still current in Santa Fe during the last century. In the 1840s, the bigoted journalist Josiah Gregg made fun of Vicar Ortiz's superstition for his having included this miraculous story of the cut wrists in a sermon to his equally stupid Mexican congregation.

* * *

Soon after Don Fernando's tactical move at San Felipe pueblo on its high mesa, and which Governor Vargas evidently acknowledged as a wise one, the latter then assigned him to lead an expedition into the western Jémez region, where its Indians had risen up and killed their padre following the revolt of Lucas Naranjo in the north Tewa countryside. On July 30, 1696, he and his men engaged the Jémez warriors in fierce combat at El Cañon de San Diego, after which the whole tribe fled west into the Navajo country. But there was still that Apache problem in the Middle Rio Grande Valley just south of his Bernalillo. For this reason the Franciscans built a church here just prior to 1700 as *La Misión de Nuestro Padre San Francisco y Población de Españoles de Bernalillo*. Here, while it was being constructed, on February 24, 1699, Don Fernando and Martín Hurtade, his brother-in-law, stood as witnesses for a Martín-Montoya wedding; his second eldest son, Pedro de Chaves, was the notary at the pre-nuptial investigations.

But the clamor was such, by those families so anxious to repossess their old estates further south, that governor Vargas found it most necessary to initiate a campaign against the Apaches. For by March of 1704 these "pagan" Indians had stampeded and stolen much of the livestock belonging to Don Fernando and his many overcrowded neighbors. In this same month, after an army of soldiers and colonists had been assembled in Bernalillo, Don Diego came down from Santa Fe to lead the expedition himself. On March 30, after a Mass was duly celebrated, they set out to drive the Apaches for good from the entire south valley. But suddenly the brave governor was taken gravely ill and was rushed back to Bernalillo on the 2nd of April. *Here he died some days later, presumably in Don Fernando's own residence, after having dictated his last will and testament; for the witnesses who signed it were Don Fernando and his eldest son Bernardo.*

But where was the great nobleman buried? Was he interred in the small church of Don Fernando's Bernalillo, the exact location of which is no longer known, with the intention of moving the remains to Santa Fe later on? What is more likely, the body was taken to the capital for burial due to its relative proximity. But, again, where? Was it in the small tower chapel of the Casas Reales where the Remedios standard was kept, or else inside the temporary church of San Francisco near the north wall on the road to Tesuque which he had built since his arrival? Neither of the two places exist anymore, nor is their exact location known. Or was he interred on the raised site of the original 1629 parish church of Padre Benavides which the Tanos had torn down following the Revolt, and where he himself had planned to rebuild it as a throne to La Conquistadora? If so, either those who completed the latter by 1717 left no record, or else such a record became lost. (The first two Burial Books of Santa Fe, 1693-1726, disappeared long ago.)

Even after his death, misfortune had followed the unlucky and debt-ridden nobleman of Madrid's noblest family. Whereas in other cities in Spain or Spanish America a great monument would still honor the last resting place of such a noteworthy man, New Mexico's traditional abobe memory had swallowed up the dust and ashes of her greatest Governor and Captain-General without leaving a trace.

7. *Albuquerque, 1706, Bernalillo*

The war against the Apaches which Governor Vargas had barely initiated must have been kept up with successful sallies which finally drove out the invaders by the following year of 1705. For by now Don Fernando's crowded neighbors had been moving down to the sites of their former homesteads. One of his sons, Antonio, already headed a squad stationed in Atrisco. Nearby, the former *estancia* of Don Fernando's wife's grandmother, Doña Luisa de Montoya (or Trujillo) had filled up with enough people to create a sizable village, and here in the following year of 1706 a new governor, Don Francisco Cuervo y Valdés, saw fit to found what he called the Villa of San Francisco de Alburquerque, so naming it after a Duke of this title who was the current Viceroy of New Spain in Mexico City. The saintly title, San Francisco Xavier, was after the name-saint of that Francisco de Trujillo whose *estancia* had occupied the site before the Pueblo Revolt; but it coincidentally suggested the governor's own given name as well as the Viceroy's, and the latter promptly changed it to San Felipe in honor of his Spanish monarch.

As for the ancient Native American dwellers of the valley, ever since the two Vargas *Entradas* of 1692 and 1693, the Tiwa Indians of Puaray, Sandía and Alameda had abandoned their pueblos, having fled to the Hopi villages in the far western desert. (It was not until some sixty years later that a few of their descendants would return, and, joined by some *genízaro*[4] families, start the present pueblo called Sandía with its new Mission of San Antonio which was begun in 1771.) Hence there had been that much more land for Spanish folks to occupy after leaving Don Fernando's property in 1705, from the central and southern

4. This term had various meanings in New Spain, but in New Mexico it had a very specific one, to be treated later with the *mestizos*. See pgs. 127-28.

portion of the present Bernalillo to Alameda, and then as far as an Albuquerque soon to be.

* * *

As for Don Fernando's own Bernalillo, its church of San Francisco continued to serve some few people living there until the whole place was sold to the Santa Ana Indians, as we shall soon see. Meanwhile his four eldest children had been getting married, then moving down to the Atrisco and Albuquerque areas after the Apaches were driven out in 1705. He himself would soon do likewise, and presumably for a very special reason, a most sorrowful one. The year after Governor Vargas had died at his home, his eldest son Bernardo, his dear "Bernalillo," suffered a terrible accident in mid-November of 1705. The women of the Chaves household had gone down to the river to do their laundering, as was the custom, and with an armed youth of the household to guard them should any stray Apaches be around. He was a very young first cousin named Juan Gallegos, the orphan son of Catarina Hurtado, a younger sister of Bernardo's own mother. To play an Indian-scare prank on them all, Bernardo stole through the willow thickets and suddenly stood up with an Apache yell, when young Gallegos spun around and shot him dead.

One can hardly imagine Don Fernando's grief when on the 19th his eldest son was buried by the padre inside the little church. One can see how much his heart was hurting in a brief note he sent to Governor Cuervo about his great loss: "I give thanks to God that His Divine Majesty has rewarded me with this burden by losing a son such as the one I have lost . . ." It shows how his sorely troubled mind scrambled his deep faith and profound sorrow together as he wrote these lines.

Right after this he sold his ancestral land, or what had been left of it after former partitions in his father's day, and with the rest of his unmarried sons and daughters moved down to Atrisco. His son Antonio was already there, in command of a small squad; because the latter was ailing at the time, his father requested to fill his post for the time being. The land that he sold, what with all the past memories of a once great Chaves El Tunque grant, besides the recent sad one of his eldest heir's tragic death, passed on to a new owner not bearing the Chaves name. Yet it was not to a complete stanger, for the purchaser was Don Fernando's brother-in-law, Manuel Baca, whose adjacent property to the south he had inherited from his own father, Cristóbal Baca. This and other close relationships now prompt another break here, and quite a necessary one, in connection with a new Bernalillo which now came into being. It brings together the past and current intimate ties between the old pioneer Baca family and those of Don Fernando Durán y Chaves and his wife Doña Lucía Hurtado de Salas y Trujillo.

As shown at the beginning, the wife of the first New Mexico Chaves had been a Vaca, or Baca, bearing the grandparental name of Isabel de Bohórques. She had two much younger brothers: Antonio Baca, who had come as a little boy and as an adult was beheaded in 1643 after the Governor Rosas murder affair, and Alonso Baca, born in New Mexico, who apparently married a *mestiza-mulata* of Analco (for being cuter than the Spanish females we suppose). We do not know her name, and we have this information from family recollections as late as 1768 and 1770. This couple had a son named Cristóbal Baca, named after his grandfather, the original Vaca of 1600.

This Cristóbal Baca came to marry a daughter of Diego de Trujillo, who was the great-grandfather of Don Fernando's wife Lucía Hurtado de Salas, as will be shown in more detail when we come to her own ancestry. Among Cristóbal Baca's children were Manuel Baca who bought Don Fernando's Bernalillo property and was married to Doña Lucía's adopted sister, María de Salazar, and Catarina Baca who had married an Antonio Gallegos, a man who had come up from Parral in New Spain sometime before the 1680 Pueblo Revolt. As said before, Manuel Baca had inherited his father Cristóbal's estate just south of Don Fernando's Bernalillo and where he moved back in 1705 after the Apaches had been driven out of the valley.

But his was not the only family which, as we have seen, had been waiting for this opportunity for the past ten years at the original Bernalillo of Don Fernando. Several of them, as said before, settled further south at a place which made the founding of Albuquerque possible, while others spread still further down the Rio Grande valley. Those who settled closer by around Manuel Baca's estate were families related to him by blood or marriage, such as the Gallegos and the Montoyas. And among them were three brothers-in-law of Don Fernando. But we are not finished with this large group's intricate relationships.

Of more particular interest here, two grand-daughters of Manuel Baca, by an unmarried daughter of his named Juana Baca, were Juana *la Moza* (the Younger) and Antonia who came to marry two of Don Fernando's sons, Francisco de Chaves and Antonio de Chaves respectively. To complicate matters more, Manuel Baca had another daughter, named Josefa Baca, who outdid her sister Juana by the six natural children, all Bacas, which she had at her prosperous ranch of Pajarito near Isleta. These are pointed out because several of them eventually married Chaves folks of their own generation.

What also brought on this break here is the curious fact that Manuel Baca, after his own large family and those of the inter-related Gallegos and Montoyas had turned his inherited estate into a village, chose the name Bernalillo as its designation. Was it because he recalled Don Fernando's recent grief when the latter's son Bernardo, also Baca's own nephew, met such a tragic end, and at the hands of another nephew of both men, Juan Gallegos?

As to the ultimate fate of Don Fernando's original Bernalillo, it was Manuel Baca's youngest daughter María Magdalena Baca, married to Diego Antonio Montoya, who must have inherited it and lived there, for decades later her son Nereo Montoya, after his mother's death, sold the entire vacated property to the Santa Ana Indians. During the preceding interval Don Fernando's church of San Francisco had continued to serve the last few people living there, but only visited by the friar of the pueblo of San Felipe or the one from Zia. Then it had been abandoned by the time Nereo Montoya sold the entire property, as just said. Meanwhile, well before the families in Don Fernando's original Bernalillo had dwindled away, the local Franciscan padre had taken up his residence in Baca's new Bernalillo while his companion had taken up his in Albuquerque. This was around the year 1718 when they were building their respective parish churches at both places in that same year—the year when Don Fernando's son Antonio de Chaves married Manuel Baca's grand-daughter Antonia Baca, and whose pre-nuptial investigations provide us with a scandalous, if somewhat amusing story, which will be told when its time comes.

8. *A Good Man's Last Days*

Coming back to Don Fernando with his sorrowful losses, he could have been feeling his own end approaching at this new home in Atrisco among most of his children. Folks in those times, and for generations later, made their wills only when they thought that death was near, and so he wrote his last will and testament on February 11, 1707. Here is where he named all of his ten children according to their ages, ending with "Pedro Gómez Durán my youngest, and all of whom I do acknowledge and are, as I have said, legitimate children and of my lawful wife." He did not die, however. Three years and a couple of months later, on December 4, 1711, he was a witness for the pre-nuptial investigations of an Albuquerque Varela-Romero couple.

But by now he had been living more and more in the past, as we gather from an unexpected violent reaction of his which took place in the following year of 1712; it also suggests that he was quite well at the time. A brief and milder spell of this sort had taken hold of him many years before at El Paso del Norte when, brooding over the treachery of all his Chaves brethren, he had reached back to his earliest known ancestor to name his last son Pedro Gómez. Now, twenty years after the resettlement of his homeland, everything was so different from what he had known prior to the great Pueblo Revolt. There were many new people with different backgrounds and outlook, like those who had come from the Valley of Mexico in 1694, as well as those later arrivals from the Mines of Zacatecas in the following summer. Even the Vargas recruits who had been born in different parts of Spain were somehow "different," although closer to his own feelings; in fact, he expected his three girls to marry some of them, which at least one did.

As for his grown-up boys, they were marrying women from the older New Mexico families, but not from the best ones in certain cases. Good old folks like the Carvajals and López Holguíns of his maternal heritage had petered out during the long exile prior to the reconquest of the land. He also recalled the Domínguez de Mendozas as preferable prospects for his sons but then shuddered at the very thought. He had come to like many of the new so-called *españoles* from the Valley of Mexico, but, unfortunately, their fine daughters had been much too young for his already marriageable sons. All in all, he must have felt himself to be the last of his New Mexico's unadulterated Spaniards, unless his mother and grandmother had been from among the "restored" ones of New Spain, something he most likely knew nothing about. And so, what troubled him the most was the fact that some descendants of the old colonial families, of those whom he had always considered as being of a lower mixed class, were now proudly acting like big lords in civic affairs as well as in the military. What a miserable kingdom, he could have been repeating to himself, even if the old miseries brought about by former evil governors were now things of the past.

In short, we have been witnessing the universal reaction of an older generation when radical changes, those especially which come about in the wake of major disturbances and wars, looks upon the new generation as a lost one. This is what brought old Don Fernando's temper to a boil in that year of 1712, when a certain Juan González was appointed *alcalde mayor* of Albuquerque. One day he savagely attacked this younger man without the least provocation, declaring that he wanted no Indian over him as mayor. He further called him *un perro mulato* (a mulatto dog), adding that he had called his father the same thing without having the charge denied. As he started to beat up the blameless fellow, he was restrained by two other men who were present. Later that day, two of his sons, Antonio and Francisco, went after González, but they, too, were constrained by a crowd which had gathered around. González in turn filed a complaint with the governor in Santa Fe, who sent down an official with orders to place the three Chaves culprits under arrest and to hear the case.

The affair must have created quite a stir among the several Chaves in-laws all the way from Bernalillo to Isleta, since the governor also authorized the *alcaldes* of Isleta, Albuquerque and Bernalillo to muster their small citizen-squads and hold them in readiness for any violent outbreaks. Days later the entire council of Albuquerque went out to execute the order of arrest as Don Fernando and some of his family were returning from a visit to Isleta. His property was also embargoed according to law, while he and his two guilty sons were placed in house arrest at the home of an in-law. During the ensuing trial, several witnesses corroborated the González charges, adding further that old Don Fernando had also called him "*un perro Indio Griego,*" meaning an Indo-Greek dog.[1]

Now, this Juan González belonged to an original New Mexico family, the paternal and maternal ancestors of which had been a Portuguese *alférez* named Sebastián González and a Greek armorer from Crete called Juan Griego (a fellow townsman of El Greco, and whose respective surnames the Spaniards were unable to spell or pronounce, hence their appellations as "Greeks"). Both of them had been prominent and respected pioneer colonists, but Don Fernando

1. He was also using the term *griego* in the sense of "foreigner" as was the old custom in Spain, and from which *gringo* was derived to denote outsiders, especially the English.

evidently knew that a goodly dose of *mestizo-mulato* genes had crept in somewhere into Juan Gonzáles's ancestry. At any rate, his had been honorable folks in the main who had previously inhabited the country north of Santa Fe, so that Don Fernando's rudeness and crass misconduct can only be explained by this senile preoccupation with the past and with the current radical changes in daily life among the younger generation.

Juan González suddenly dropped the charges, stating that he wanted to be a good friend of Don Fernando. Or had he received orders to do so from Santa Fe? For in presenting this petition he was accompanied by a group of high officials, so that it looks as though the governor had woken up to the fact that Don Fernando, as the petition states, had at least nominal titles of High Sheriff and Regent of the Kingdom. Such are the ways of politics, then as now.

This is the last we hear of Don Fernando Durán y Chaves the Second, now the one and only progenitor of the New Mexico Chaves clan. Four years later, in 1716, his wife was referred to as a widow. The first Albuquerque church was yet to be built on the west end of the plaza, else he would have been buried in it as the prominent citizen that he was. Instead of the preceding acrid episode, one should have expected a final curtain call most resplendent with a glorifying of God on high and a call for peace to men of good will, in accordance with all his sentiments as expressed in many a declaration of his in the past. One likes to think that his beloved New Mexico did put on a show the day he died, as her adobe-flecked atmosphere and colorful features lit up the sky with the red and gold of Castile as the sun itself went down, but eventually making his dust her very adobe own without leaving a trace as in the case of his friend Don Diego de Vargas.

9. *Another Helpmate, Soap Operas*

His faithful wife Doña Lucía survived him by more than thirteen years in the care of some of her children in Atrisco. There was a suit against her and her sons regarding livestock at this period, which ended with an apology to the plaintiffs. She finally passed away on February 3, 1729. As in the case of the former Chaves wives and mothers, she and her own family background now call for full recognition. But now the ancestral line of Doña Lucía Hurtado de Salas y Trujullo is quite longer than the former ones, particularly on the female side since women in those times got married at a very early age.

However, instead of lacking full foliage as so many family trees grow, there are more branches and sprigs in her paternal and maternal lines to furnish us with more than the usual color and drama. On the Hurtado paternal side, there are more vivid pictures of the church-state crises in which her Chaves mate's own forebears had been involved; on the maternal one, there are the kind of sexual situations and episodes which our current soap operas put forth as original plots. First we start with Doña Lucía's parents.

Her father, Andrés Hurtado, was a native of the city of Zacatecas and a newcomer in 1661, being only thirty-three years old when he finds first mention in that year. By this time he was already married to a fine lady named Doña Bernardina de Salas y Trujillo, and they had five small children. They were living in the Sandía *Alcaldía* while he held the *encomienda* of Santa Ana Pueblo and others nearby, hence he was a neighbor of the first Don Fernando Durán y Chaves at his own Tunque *estancia;* like him, we also learn, he was a good friend of the Franciscan missionaries. He had also been chosen as a regent and procurator general of the Kingdom, all of which could mean that, as a young man of good background, he had come as a trusted officer of some good governor like Don Luis de Guzmán in 1647 or later, some years prior to the arrival of the infamous Governor López de Mendizábal. For it was this bitter enemy of the friars who began persecuting him as he had the first Don Fernando for the same reasons. One case we know of took place in 1661, when Mendizábal made him bring his entire family to Santa Fe in the dead of winter. The oldest of his five children was only nine; one girl had a foot frozen along the way while his wife suffered a miscarriage. One of the children, Lucía, was to become the bride of the junior Don Fernando Durán y Chaves.

Nor do we know what indignities Hurtado suffered under the next evil governor, Peñalosa. The last we hear of him is a couple of years later, in 1664, when he was still living at his old homestead as a captain of cavalry as well as the *síndico* of the Franciscans. He was dead by 1680 when his widow Bernardina with a married son, the junior Andrés Hurtado, joined the other Río Abajo refugees in their flight to El Paso del Norte. Among these other families were her daughter Lucía and her Chaves mate with their own four little children.

As already said, Andrés Hurtado's wife was Doña Bernardina de Salas y Trujillo (or else *Ossorio* or *Orozco,* names used only once each, and presumably reaching back to some Trujillo forebear). Anyway, her own line is as long and complicated as the full name she always used. Her father had been a Francisco de Trujillo about whose career we know next to nothing, except that his wife was a woman named Luisa or Lucía de Montoya. (These two similar first names were interchangeable among the New Mexico colonists in those days.) Francisco himself was the only son of a Diego de Trujillo and his wife Catarina Vásquez, Diego being a native of Mexico City who first appears as an *alferez* and stockman nineteen or twenty years of age. In 1641 he was in a military escort to and from Mexico City. The next we hear of him is in 1661, when he gave his age as forty-eight and was living at his *estancia* four leagues from the pueblo of Sandía, and which he called El Paraje de las Huertas. At this time he was also the *alcalde* for the Zuñi and Hopi pueblos which he visited on occasion. In this capacity he was accused of having punished some Indians for not having attended Mass, and of having as slaves some Apaches which those Pueblo Indians had captured, and for this he was exiled to Mexico City.

Two sons-in-law of his at this time were Cristóbal Baca and Andrés Hurtado. (This Baca's wife used the name Ana Moreno de Lara for whatever reason, while Hurtado, married to Bernardina, was actually Trujillo's grandson-in-law.) All this we get from the Inquisition's trial of that Governor Mendizábal who likewise had persecuted Trujillo because of his devotion to the Franciscans. Hence those accusations mentioned before appear to have been false ones, since he was back in the following year, having returned in the soldier-escort which brought the next evil governor, Peñalosa. In this year of 1662 he gave his age as fifty, now a *sargente major* in his Sandía district as well as the *teniente de gobernador* for the Río Abajo, and once again the *alcalde* for the Zuñi pueblos. Apparently he had avoided incurring Peñalosa's enmity for the nonce.

All this also brings up a supposition in connection with those false accusations made during Mendizábal's Inquisition trial when he was previously *alcalde* at Zuñi. For it is the only explanation that we have for certain aspects in his granddaughter Bernardina's family as the wife of Andrés Hurtado. Instead of taking Apache slaves as he had been accused of doing, he had taken three tiny girls born of one or the other Zuñi woman from casual encounters with a couple of Hispanic philanderers, his intention being to rear them as "true Christians" for their being part Spanish. One of the three, later known as Juana de Ynojos, must have had a father by this name, since we know that at least one Ynojos fellow was prone to do such things. The other two, subsequently known as Juana and María de

Salazar, could have been the spawn of a Bartolomé de Salazar, or Ledesma, who had preceded Diego de Trujillo as *alcalde* of Zuñi and was also known for his philandering. The three of them, reared by Doña Bernardina de Salas y Trujillo, came to be regarded as "sisters" of Doña Lucía Hurtado de Salas, wife of our Don Fernando Durán y Chaves.

By 1669 Diego de Trujillo was a *maese de campo* as well as the syndic for the mission friars. He was still living when the 1680 Pueblo Revolt broke out, but two years later is mentioned as having died while on a trip to Casas Grandes in New Spain. As mentioned at the start, he had only one son, Francisco de Trujillo, who had married Luisa or Lucía de Montoya. As for the origins of Diego's own wife, they are cloudy at best. Catarina Vásquez had given her age as forty-eight in 1669 and Santa Fe as her place of birth. What we know is that there had been a Francisco Vásquez, twenty-eight years old, the son of Alonso Alfrán and a native of Cartaya in Spain, who had come in 1598. Most likely a daughter of his was an old Doña Bernardina Vásquez living at her *estancia* of Los Cerrillos near Santa Fe in 1660. We can only guess that Catarina Vásquez was very closely related to her, most likely her daughter since her only son Francisco de Trujillo passed on the rare name "Bernardina" to his own child, who became the wife of Andrés Hurtado.

* * *

Here is where the main soap opera really starts in earnest, in Doña Bernardina's background on her Montoya mother's side. Francisco de Trujillo's wife, Doña Luisa de Montoya, was a daughter of one Diego de Montoya and María de Vera, her father being a son of Bartolomé de Montoya, a native of Sevilla, who had come with his large family back in 1600. But it is María de Vera's story which contributes most to the drama. Her own father had been that Diego de Vera, the Canary Islander from Tenerife, who had arrived in Santa Fe prior to 1622 when, on January 16, he married María de Abendaño; for this wedding, we may recall, the bride's aunt Doña Isabel de Bohórques and Governor Sotelo had stood as witnesses. The happy pair consequently had two baby girls named Petronila and María de Vera. Three years afterward, toward the end of 1625, Fray Alonso de Benavides, a Canary Islander himself, arrived in Santa Fe as the new Franciscan *Custodio* with the added powers of Commissary for the Holy Office. Awed perhaps by the presence of this powerful countryman, Diego de Vera soon disclosed to Padre Benavides that he was a bigamist who still had a wife back in Tenerife.

The Commissary promptly started a trial, and as a result of it had the culprit taken to Mexico City for shipment back to his wife in the Canaries. This trial, as found in the Inquisition records, provides us with the kind of genealogy which, as Dr. Scholes regretted, we would have had for the Chaves dynasty had any of its members been tried by the Holy Office for some serious breach of church law. Hence we outline Diego de Vera's here as part and parcel of the ancestry of Doña Lucía Hurtado de Salas y Trujillo as the wife of Don Fernando Durán y Chaves.

Diego's parents were Pedro de Vera Perdomo and María de Betancurt, residents of the City of La Laguna on the island of Tenerife. His paternal grandparents were Hernán Martín Baena, a native of Jerez de la Frontera on the mainland, and Catarina García, native of La Laguna. The maternal grandparents were Antonio Pérez, born on the island of La Graciosa, and Catarina Aponte, native of Garachico on Tenerife. As just pointed out, Diego de Vera was shipped back to his wife as the penalty for his crime.

As for his poor bereft second wife, María de Abendaño, who was left alone with her tiny Vera girls, Petronila and María, she later married an Antonio de Salas, born in Mexico City, who was the stepson of Pedro Lucero de Godoy, an upright original settler with a superior background. But his Salas stepson turned out to be just the opposite, at least in his later years. In 1639 he had been a member of the Santa Fe *Cabildo,* and in 1642 was employed as a guard for that evil Governor Rosas when the latter was murdered; what part he played in it is anybody's guess. But much later, in 1664, when he held the *encomienda* of Pojoaque Pueblo, where he resided with his wife María de Abendaño with their one son Simón de Salas—and also her now adult Vera daughters, Petronila and María—he was formally accused of having sexual relations with his stepdaughter Petronila, already married to a Pedro Romero. What the outcome of this lurid episode was we do not know. Neither Antonio de Salas nor his son Simón appear in the 1680 refugee lists, perhaps having died or left New Mexico well before this.

As for poor Petronila, whatever the degree of her adulterous guilt had been, she and her entire Romero family were massacred by the Pojoaque Indians in that terrible August of 1680.

Her younger sister María de Vera had first married a Manuel Jorge, a Greek armorer who had come in 1600. (Another such was that Juan Griego mentioned before during old Don Fernando's altercation with Juan González.) This Manuel Jorge and María de Vera had a son and three daughters, all subsequently using the surname Jorge de Vera. After Jorge's death, María then married a widower named Diego de Montoya, by whom she had our Luisa de Montoya who came to marry Francisco de Trujillo. Their one daughter Bernardina became the wife of Andrés Hurtado. As it looks, Trujillo had given her this name after that possible Vásquez grandmother at Los Cerrillos. What really is more intriguing is Bernardina's own use of "Salas" in her surname as Bernardina de Salas y Trujillo. This evidently refers to that lecherous Antonio de Salas who had been her maternal grandmother's second husband. Perhaps, after such a long time when family memories became muddled, she did think that Salas was her real forebear and, ignorant of that fellow's degenerate nature and conduct, took to the Salas surname because she liked the sound of it.

Or did she actually come from an adulterous child of Salas and poor Petronila de Vera, and who had been reared by her aunt María de Vera? *Quién sabe?*

* * *

This is how Bernardina's eldest daughter, Lucía Hurtado de Salas y Trujillo, then got her full name: "Lucía" from her grandmother Lucía (or Luisa) de Montoya, "Hurtado" from her father Andrés, and "Salas y Trujillo" from her mother. And she liked to use the full long name to distinguish herself from three younger "sisters" of hers, Isabel de Salazar who had married Juan Lucero de Godoy, María de Salazar who was the wife of Manuel Baca, and Josefa de Ynojos who married Diego Montoya.

While we are on this fascinating subject of given names, and as a final bow to our dear Doñá Lucía Hurtado de Salas y Trujillo, we can speculate on the names her ten Chaves children received in baptism. For it does look as though she and Don Fernando took turns in selecting most of them. First at Bernalillo before 1680: *Bernardo* points to Doña Lucía's mother Bernardina, while *Pedro* was Don Fernando's own choice recalling his own grandfather, Don Pedro Durán y Chaves; next, *Antonio,* as his mother's choice, seems to go back to that Antonio de Salas whom she regarded as her ancestor; then came the first girl, *Isabel,* her father's turn for recalling his grandmother, Isabel de Bohórques.—Then, at El Paso del Norte following the 1680 Pueblo Revolt: *Francisco,* his mother's turn for honoring her father Francisco Trujillo; next, *Luis,* her choice again to honor her grandmother Luisa de Montoya.

For by this time it looks as though Don Fernando, preoccupied with more serious matters concerning the colony in exile, had left these things for his wife to decide, the latter naming the next three children *Nicolás, María* and *Catarina* for whatever reasons she had in mind. But finally, with his now increasing preoccupation with the past as all of his many Chaves relatives were abandoning their homeland, Don Fernando set his foot down by repeating his second son's Pedro name when he christened his tenth and last child as *Pedro Gómez,* thereby emphasizing for himself and his family the revered founder of a dynasty which by now was becoming so sadly shattered.

All of these seven sons of his make up the next, and final, long section about a once more proliferating Chaves Clan.

PART THREE

The Seven Sons of Don Fernando

Detail from 1758 Miera y Pacheco map of settlements.

Courtesy, Museum of New Mexico.

Prelude on the Three Daughters

This main heading omits the three daughters of Don Fernando Durán y Chaves, but not for chauvinistic reasons since up until now the female side has been fully acknowledged. The main reason for it is that, while all these three Chaves sisters left no descendants to pass down the old family name, their total issue consisted of only two surviving girls which one of them had. But their persons and marriages must be treated, and from here on we begin using titles and full names as they appear in the marital records. Tiresome and obtrusive as they may seem, they are most necessary to illustrate the pathetic efforts being made by certain individuals to distinguish themselves as true *españoles* from what they considered the mixed common herd. There are also scandalous and comical episodes throughout to relieve the tediousness of such accounts, since life would be dull if everybody was a saint.

---

1. The eldest one, *Doña Isabel de Chaves,* while living at her father's Bernalillo, first married a widower named Jacinto Peláez in 1700. He was a native of Villanueva de las Montañas in Asturias, the son of Gonzalo Peláez and Elvira Méndez, who had first married Margarita Gómez Robledo of that noted Toledo family often mentioned before, and by whom he had only one daughter named Maria (who in 1710 married another Spaniard from Galicia, Juan Fernández de la Pedrera).[1] Jacinto Peláez was also one of the several Spain-born soldiers whom Governor Vargas had recruited for the Reconquest, but he was dead prior to 1705 when his widow Doña Isabel married again, he having left her with one baby daughter named Jacinta after himself; she, as Doña Jacinta Peláez, daughter of the *capitán* Don Jacinto Peláez, deceased, and Doña Isabel Chaves, married Antonio de Luna on May 29, 1718. This Luna was the son "of parents not known" living in Bernalillo, yet identified as her second and third cousins, and they were granted a dispensation because the bride was orphaned of her father while there was a dearth in the region of suitable males whereby she was in danger of "marrying beneath her station!" Incidentally, Luna had to work fifteen days in building the Bernalillo church and to donate five hundred adobes for the one

1. GENEALOGY: **María Peláez**, María Francisca Fernández de la Pedrera, Manuel Alarí, José María Alarí, María Dolores Alarid, Romualdo Roybal, Nicolasa Roybal, Fr. A. Chávez.

going up in Albuquerque, while the bride was to sweep either church during the ten days preceding the fiesta vespers!—The eldest of their children was Domingo Luna who in 1745 married a Josefa Lucero by whom he had several children.[2] After her Luna husband died in 1729, Jacinta married an Antonio Montoya in 1737, and she herself passed away at Tomé in 1766.

As for her mother Doña Isabel de Chaves, she had gotten married a second time; on January 14, 1705, the said Doña Isabel, widow of Jacinto Peláez and daughter of Don Fernando de Chaves and Doña Lucía Hurtado, was united to another native of Spain named Don Salvador de Mata, the son of Pedro de Mata and Isabel Martínez, but whose specific birthplace was not given. They had two children, a girl and a boy; Margarita de Mata, born on October 5, 1705, who married Bernabé Baca in May 1718 (the same year and month when her Peláez half-sister married Antonio de Luna), and Pedro de Mata, born August 12, 1708, who must have died since no people of this surname appear in any records for decades to come.

Widowed once more, prior to 1718, after her second brief marriage, Isabel was ready for a third one. As Doña Isabel Durán y Chaves, widow of Don Salvador (or Baltasar?) de Mata, the daughter of Don Fernando Durán y Chaves and Doña Lucía Hurtado, she was asked for in marriage that same year by Don Eusebio Rael de Aguilar. He was a soldier of Santa Fe and only twenty-four years old. Elsewhere we learn that he was the son of Alonso Rael de Aguilar, a recruit from Murcia in Spain who had been Governor Vargas' chief aide and secretary throughout the Reconquest campaigns. Eusebio was at least ten years younger than his prospective bride, and there is no record of the wedding ever having taken place; but even if it had, there were no children to complement the one perhaps deceased boy and the two married girls whom Isabel had by those other two vaunted Dons from Spain. No doubt, her father Don Fernando, while disappointed by the lack of male heirs, must have most heartily approved of his eldest girl's two Spain-born husbands.

---

2. The second girl, as *Doña María Durán y Chaves,* daughter of Don Fernando Durán y Chaves and Doña Lucía Hurtado, had been asked for in 1708 by one Juan

2. GENEALOGY: **Isabel D. y Chaves,** Jacinta Peláez, Domingo Luna, Antonio Luna, José Enrique Luna, Toribio Luna, María Encarnación Luna. Eugenio Chávez, Fabián Chávez, Fr. A. Chávez.

Tafoya de Altamirano of Santa Fe. But the marriage did not materialize because of a scandalous impediment brought up against the prospective groom, and which will be divulged shortly for its having its own special significance. Finally Doña María did get married a couple of years later prior to 1711, when she finds mention as the wife of an Antonio de Ulibarrí, there being no record extant of this marriage, and one which Don Fernando might not have approved of during his strong preoccupation with the past, along with his concern about the new kind of folks invading his "miserable kingdom." This Ulibarrí was a native of San Juan de la Paz in Mexico City, his parents there being José Enríquez de los Reyes and María de Ynojos. In 1713, referred to as Doña María Chaves Hurtado, she and her Ulibarrí husband were witnesses for a family wedding. Later they went to live in Santa Fe. But apparently they had no children of their own, having reared an orphan girl named Rosa de Armijo, the child of José Durán de Armijo and Manuela Velásquez of Santa Fe, and who in 1732 was suing Ulibarrí for her adoptive mother's inheritance. This indicates that María was dead well before this time.

---

3. The third daughter, as *Doña Catarina Chaves,* daughter of Don Fernando Durán y Chaves and Doña Lucía Hurtado, married a young widower by the name of Matías de Miranda in Albuquerque in December 1711. He was a native of Llerena del Real de Sombrerete near Zacatecas, the son of Benito de Miranda and Doña María de Aguilar. His first wife had died the previous year, presumably down in Zacatecas. Here Don Fernando must have given his heartiest approval, not so much because of the groom's place of origin, but because he was actually the younger brother of a local Franciscan padre, Fray Antonio de Miranda, who came all the way from his Ácoma Mission to perform the wedding. This was witnessed by the bride's sister María de Chaves and her Ulibarrí husband, and by her brother Francisco Chaves and Catarina Jaramillo (wife of their uncle Martín Hurtado). However, there is no hint anywhere of any Miranda children from this union.

Finally, one must not forget that fourth but clandestine daughter, *Clara*

Chaves, who was hinted at a long while back. In 1708, when that Tafoya Altamirano fellow in Santa Fe asked to marry Don Fernando's second daughter María, a most serious impediment was brought up by this Clara Chaves, now married to a Juan de la Mora Pineda. She testified that she was commonly known to be the "*hija bastarda del capitán Don Fernando de Chaves,*" and that she previously had had carnal relations with the prospective groom, a fact she said was well known by his own brother Cristóbal Tafoya and his wife.[3] Unfortunately, the name of Clara's mother, who also testified that Don Fernando had made her pregnant as a girl, was not recorded—for us to get some idea about his erotic tastes, while wishfully thinking that this had been his one and only deviation of this sort.

Clara and her husband had only one son, Miguel de la Mora Pineda, who got married in Santa Fe in 1718; but his full name did not survive for long. Strangely enough, neither did the Peláez and Mata ones as we have seen. But the Chaves one did a-plenty, as will be shown when we proceed to look into the lives of Don Fernando's seven sons.

* * *

From now on we ordinarily leave out the "Don" prefix unless when specified on occasion, for it no longer had its previous connotation of implied nobility. Don Fernando himself must have winced whenever he heard the Bacas, Luceros, Montoyas, and other leading families applying the once exclusive title to themselves. But this was the practice of the times. Even the *español* designation, once taken for granted before 1680, was being used more and more by people having Amerind infusions in the not too distant past, hence not quite fully restored Spaniards. It is by way of illustration that we bring in all such expressions as contained in the documents, along with the full appellation of Durán y Chaves which some successive members of the clan kept on recalling as a sign of ethnic distinction or superiority.

For the same reasons, and just as legitimately, others who bore just as old and honorable colonial surnames persisted in distinguishing themselves as the pure *españoles* which they honestly deemed themselves to be. For, while the preceding

3. *Copula ilicita* between persons related by blood or marriage was then a serious impediment which had to be revealed in conscience.

century's *mestizo-mulatos* had brought their own surnames acquired down in New Spain, the *genízaro* servants of this new one—children of assorted Plains tribes—were adopting the surnames of their local masters, including the Chaves one of the sons of Don Fernando who individually make the third part of this narrative.

I. Bernardo Durán y Chaves

Francisca Mízquia y Lucero

A Fond Father's Tragic Loss

Acting as a pre-marital witness in Santa Fe in the years 1694 and 1695, Bernardo gave his age as twenty-one and twenty-two respectively, his birth around 1672 being just about right for the eldest of Don Fernando's four children born in Bernalillo prior to the Pueblo Revolt of 1680. Apparently he had stayed on in Santa Fe as a soldier of the Presidio when his father and the rest of the family moved down to the old Bernalillo estate around this time. Then his squadron was sent on temporary duty to El Paso del Norte sometime during 1698, where he signed as a witness in August of this year. There he fell in love with a maid named *Francisca de Mísquia,* whom he as Don Bernardo de Chaves married on January 2, 1699 (the date recorded in the briefer *diligencia matrimonial* made in Santa Fe).

Don Fernando would most certainly have approved of this bride because of her parentage, as we shall soon see. Shortly after this, Bernardo's military stint must have ended, for soon he was back with his wife at Bernalillo where he had been born, and where his first child was baptized in April of 1700. Exactly four years later, as we have seen, in April of 1704, he and his father Don Fernando witnessed and signed the last will of Governor Don Diego de Vargas shortly before this great gentleman passed away in their home. By this time he and Francisca already had two boys and a girl.

Then, in the following year, when playing that Apache-scare prank likewise described previously, he was accidentally shot dead by a young cousin of his, and was then buried by a most deeply grieving father on November 19, 1705.

His young widow was the daughter of the *capitãn* Lázaro de Mísquia, a Basque born in La Villa de Motrico in Guipúscoa, and whose father's name was Domingo (mother's name not mentioned). He had come to New Mexico in 1677 in charge of some convicts, when he was described as being twenty-four, tall and fair with a broad face, large forehead, and thick eyebrows. Sometime thereafter he married Donã María Lucero de Godoy, a daughter of Pedro Lucero de Godoy and Francisca Gómez Robledo, both traceable scions of two prominent pioneer families. When the Pueblo Revolt of 1680 broke out, he took an active part in the defense of Santa Fe, and subsequently was among its refugees at El Paso del Norte with his Lucero wife and two small children. These were little Francisca and a boy named Domingo after his grandfather. In the following year, Lázaro was described as having a good stature and features, a fair and ruddy complexion, with a thick reddish beard and long reddish straight hair.

Not being a New Mexico colonist officially, he did not return with the Vargas Reconquest of 1693, but settled down at El Paso del Norte where he acted as Procurator of the Kingdom in 1695. Three years later, as we have seen, his daughter Francisca became the wife of young Bernardo Durán y Chaves, and in 1705 at El Paso del Norte his soldier-son Domingo de Mízquia, referred to as a native of New Mexico, married a Juana Jurado. And so the Basque surname permanently disappeared from New Mexico. (Some possible descendants in what is now northern Mexico seem to have transformed the name into "Misquez.")

Now back once more to Bernardo's young widow Francisca and their small children. He had left her with three little ones, all born in Bernalillo: *José,* April 24, 1700; *María Manuela,* June 15, 1703; and *Juan,* February 26, 1705, who was only some eight months old when his father was killed. Their mother had next married a Juan de Ulibarrí, brother of that Antonio who married her sister-in-law María de Chaves sometime prior to 1711. These two weddings might have taken place at the same time, or else close together; and shortly thereafter, as the wife of Juan de Ulibarrí, poor Francisca felt her end approaching and drew up her last will. In it she specified that her three children, the eldest being fourteen, be placed in the care of her own people at El Paso del Norte. (Here she gave her small daughter's name as *Lucía* Manuela, whom she must have named after Bernardo's mother, but which the padre failed to record after baptizing the child.)

As for the fate of these three children, the eldest one, José de Chaves, was married and living in El Paso del Norte in 1769, which shows that his mother's will of 1714 had been carried out following her premature death. In this same year of 1769 his sister (here called *Luisa* de Chaves) was mentioned as already deceased, and their younger brother, Juan de Chaves, as residing or being present in Santa Fe at the time. The latter is evidently a Juan de Chaves, twenty-three, who in 1726 married a Bernalillo girl named Doña María (Rosa?) de San Juan, who was fourteen. The pre-nuptial document is incomplete, but she had to be a daughter of Miguel de San Juan, a native of El Paso del Norte and of "unknown parentage" (but somehow related to the Luna people of New Mexico through contacts made down there during the refugee exile of 1680-1693). He had come to Bernalillo and married an Isabel Montoya in 1710. Our Juan de Chaves must have done the same some years later, when he married the San Juan girl in 1726; a year later, also at Bernalillo, when he gave his age as twenty-four, he witnessed the marriage of Doña Margarita de Luna, evidently his sister-in-law as the daughter of Miguel de San Juan and Isabel Montoya; here he stated that he had witnessed the burial at El Paso del Norte of the first wife of the Durán fellow who was marrying Margarita de Luna.

Then we have the curt notice in the Albuquerque burial book of a María Rosa de Luna, the wife of a Juan de Chaves, who died on October 6, 1738, while her newly born baby of the same name was buried on the 12th. Is this the same couple we have been considering? And, if so, did this Juan de Chaves marry again and was actually living in Santa Fe by 1769? So far we do not know, nor if there were any children of his to pass down the name.

Bernardo's eldest son, José de Chaves, might have had sons at El Paso del Norte to perform this task, but any such descendants were lost to New Mexico just as had Don Fernando's many relatives who had abandoned their homeland after 1680. And so it looks as though Bernardo, the firstborn son of Don Fernando Durán y Chaves, contributed nothing to the furtherance of the Chaves Clan in New Mexico. This was left for some of his other six sons, starting with the next one in line, Pedro Durán y Chaves, who did so in earnest.

II. Pedro Durán y Chaves

Juana Montoya de Ynojos
Gertrudis Sánchez

1. *A Large Family and a Will*

In the latter part of the eighteenth century, an Albuquerque tradition held that the villa had been founded in 1706 by twelve families, a neat apostolic number so to speak. This is what a very old man named Juan Candelaria wrote in 1776, when he included that of Pedro Durán y Chaves among those first twelve. This was true of Pedro's own family, as we shall see, while those of his father Don Fernando and of his other brothers settled in nearby Atrisco, whether or not the river divided both places at the time. (Sometimes it changed its course to the east, along the present railroad route.)

Pedro was about twenty-five at his father's Bernalillo when, during the year 1699, the friar there had him acting as his notary for the pre-nuptial investigations. The parties in question, we must bear in mind, belonged to the many Río Abajo families crowded there and in its vicinity, all of them waiting for the Apaches to be driven out of the valley where their former homes had been. One interesting marriage was that of his cousin Elena Gallegos with Santiago Grolé, a French-born adventurer whom Governor Vargas had recruited in Mexico City among others. Another marriage, here noted for its being rather touching, was that of another close relative named María Hurtado who was designated as a *coyota* when she married an Alejo Gutiérrez; this was because her Hurtado mother, taken captive as a girl in the 1680 Pueblo Revolt, had been rescued with her acquired half-breed children by the Vargas troops in 1692.

Pedro himself got married at his father's Bernalillo on January 27, 1703. His bride, *Juana Montoya de Ynojos,* belonged to one of the several families there which were awaiting the expulsion of the Apaches. When this happened in 1705, her Montoya family moved down to Manuel Baca's new Bernalillo, while she and her Chaves husband went further down to the place which was named Albuquerque in the following year, there to be remembered as one of the founding families some seventy years later. Here Pedro became part of the small military guard, presumably at the head of it as was his brother Antonio at a similar post in Atrisco. Here also, during January of 1707, he played a part in an incident having the earmarks of a stage farce. A soldier named García, who already had two babies by a local girl, was formally accused by her brother of having reneged on his promises to marry her. Then Don Pedro de Chaves as his commanding officer, accompanied by his uncle Martín Hurtado who was the *alcalde,* went with the local padre to interview the young woman at her brother's home—and there they caught her in bed with her soldier-lover! Subsequently, Pedro was a witness at the interrogations preceding the pair's wedding on January 24.

In this connection, Pedro himself must have had a similar fling of his own. A pre-nuptial family chart of 1766 shows that the bride's father, Bernardo Vallejo by name, was the son of our Pedro de Chaves, hence an illegitimate whose mother was a Vallejo woman, or else he had been reared by a person of this name—and this slender clue to Pedro's infidelity had to be unearthed a couple of centuries later by none other than a descendant of his by at least two direct lines!

Pedro was still connected with the military prior to 1713, when he is said to have led a soldier-escort which conducted Don Felix Martínez back to Mexico City. (This man, an outsider, was acting as interim governor in 1715-1717, after which he left New Mexico for good.) In 1716 Pedro resigned his commission because of an alleged illness, yet took part in a Moqui campaign later in this same year. Twelve years after this we find him a widower with ten children when he married a *Gertrudis Sánchez* on January 22, 1728. From what we gather later on, his first Montoya wife had passed away shortly before this.

This second marriage, while posing quite a problem concerning this Sánchez woman herself, throws considerable light on the circumstances surrounding the probation of his estate in March of 1735, and the drawing-up of his last will and testament just prior to his death on December 7 of this same year. The probation suit was prompted by the fact that Pedro, about sixty-two years old at the time, was extremely ill and out of his senses besides. Here we learn that, as Don Fernando's eldest living son, he had come into possession of his father's will made in 1707; but of late, because of this same illness and mental incapacity, it had already been passed on to his brother Antonio of Atrisco as Don Fernando's next eldest son, and who at this very time "was absent from the Kingdom." Hence it looks as though Pedro's physical and mental incapacitation had been developing since a good while back.

This brings us to the will which was written up before Pedro passed away. Heading the list of his ten children, and with very particular emphasis, are his four eldest married daughters who also include their husbands: *Manuela*, wife of Sebastián Marcelino who is the administrator of the estate; *Mõncia*, wife of Antonio Baca; *Josefa*, wife of Francisco Sánchez; and *Efigenia*, wife of Jacinto Sánchez. From this and from other indications, it certainly looks as though these four adult sisters, the eldest Manuela in particular, had dictated the terms of the will to their addled parent, and with no little help from that Marcelino husband.

After this they listed the next three children, grown-up but still single; *Francisco Xavier* (whom elsewhere they called a wastrel), then *Quiteria* and *Juana*. After this came the final three of the ten children whom they designated as minors: *Diego Antonio,* age twelve; *Marís Luisa,* age ten; and *Eusebio,* age eight. These three, they added, had been placed in the care of their uncle Francisco Chaves at the time their father remarried.

Gertrudis Sánchez, the second wife of 1728 with a brood of her own, is left out of the inheritance. She purportedly had had five children by Pedro during the past seven years, but they were completely disinherited. One of them had died, but none of the four living ones are even named. (They will be identified later as found in other sources.) But why, we may ask, had the three minors by the first wife, Juana Montoya, why had they been placed in their uncle Francisco's care when their father Pedro remarried in 1728? They were all little tots at the time: only five, three, and one years of age. Had the new bride refused to take them before the marriage took place? Or had the four eldest daughters and their uncle Francisco, distrustful of the Sánchez young woman, deemed it the best course to take? If so, had Pedro's mental faculties been so impaired at this stage that he, a proud Hispanic male of superior background and upbringing, could countenance such a thing?

This could have been in the minds of his eldest married daughters when it all happened. Subsequently, when they saw how much their father's dementia had progressed by March of 1735, they took matters into their own hands by first having the estate probated, then nine months later steering his confused mind when composing the will just the way they wanted. Nor had they consulted their one adult younger brother, Francisco Xavier, for his being a spendthrift in their regard.

Before proceeding futher with this confusing and really unfortunate development, it seems nothing but right and proper at this stage to consider the departed mother whom these ten children so sorely missed, as it looks from the tenot of the entire will's wordage. Besides, as in the case of former Chaves helpmates going far back, she deserves special treatment as the faithful wife and mother she seems to have been.

2. *A Good Helpmate, Blood from Cíbola*

Doña Juana Montoya de Ynojos was the daughter of Diego de Montoya and María Josefa de Ynojos. When the Vargas colonists reached Santa Fe in late December of 1693, this Diego and his young family took refuge from the winter weather in some vacant dwelling within the Tano-occupied Villa; then they luckily managed to escape in time before the occupying Tanos decided to resist Governor Vargas who, in his turn, had to take the town by means of a bloody battle. Juana was a young girl at the time, and must have often told her own many children about that crucial event and its aftermath.

Some three years after that event, her family and that of her uncle Antonio Montoya moved down to the *estancia* of Don Fernando de Chaves called Bernalillo, where she married the latter's son Pedro in 1703. Her Pedro's mother, Doña Lucía Hurtado de Salas, had a sister named María Hurtado who was the wife of her uncle Antonio, while her own mother Josefa de Ynojos was an adopted sister of theirs. From this triple relationship she could have begun to learn how to be a wonderful wife and mother herself, as the mothers of such big families must have been in those harsh times and generations later. Especially so had been her own mother during so many similar trials of wars and exile with her Montoya husband.

On her father's side, the family line went back to her grandfather Bartolomé de Montoya, who had inherited the old San Pedro Pueblo grant at the eastern end of the original Chaves *estancia* of El Tunque from his own father, the first Diego de Montoya; the latter in turn was the son of the very first pioneer settler of this name, Bartolomé Montoya the First, who had brought his entire family of wife, three boys, and two girls far back in 1600. This good man was a native of Cantillana near Sevilla in southern Spain, twenty-eight years old at the time, the son of Francisco de Montoya, and described as being short of stature and wearing a black beard. The wife, María de Zamora, was a native of Mexico City, the daughter of Pedro de Zamora, a former mayor of Oaxaca, and his wife Agustina Abarca.

As for her maternal Ynojos line, it is altogether different from that of her Montoya father, her mother María Josefa de Ynojos being part-Zuñi Indian—from the place which Fray Marcos de Niza had called Cíbola far back in 1539. Many years later, in 1775, a self-styled "Don" José Vicente Durán y Chaves, "of unknown parentage," (hence the bastard son of some Chaves buck of Atrisco), asked to marry a certain maiden. This prospective bride was his first cousin and, as proof, Chaves deposed that Josefa de Ynojos, the wife of Diego de Montoya, and who was his great-great grandmother, was a *coyota* of Zuñi and (half) sister of an Indian named Ventura—she also being the mother of Antonio Montoya who was his great-grandfather. On the same score, he said, this Antonio Montoya's sister, Rosa Montoya, was his prospective bride's great-great grandmother. Now, the steps of descent, besides revealing that native admixture, do fit nicely on a chart, save for the lack of intervening ancestors' identities which could tell us who the wayward Chaves father of José Vicente was.

María Josefa de Ynojos, by the way, had stood as a marriage witness with Andrés Hurtado (her adoptive brother) at El Paso del Norte in 1689. As for her Ynojos surname and background, we can only make a wide guess, although not a wild one. Two Ynojos (or Yñíguez) brothers from Cartaya, Condado de Niebla in Spain, had come as soldiers with Oñate in 1598, their father being a Juan Ruíz. One of them, Sebastián Ruíz de Ynojos, was killed on the great rock of Ácoma in that same year, hence leaving no descendants. The other one, Hernando de Ynojos, continued as a most able official until his death prior to 1632. His wife was Beatríz de Bustillos from a good Mexico City family, and they had three or more sons, one of which was among the eight men beheaded in 1643 following the murder of Governor Rosas. The eldest one, Miguel de Ynojos, was as successful as his father, but prone to have children by the Indian women in any of the pueblo *alcaldías* which he served. Several Ynojos men were among the refugees of 1680 at El Paso del Norte, none of whom returned to New Mexico. But it is one of the elder ones of this group who must have engendered Josefa de Ynojos at Zuñi prior to the Pueblo Revolt.

Whatever the case may be, the mother of Doña Juana Montoya did happen to be half-Zuñi, just as were two "sisters" of hers, Isabel de Salazar and María de Salazar who had married Juan Lucero de Godoy and Manuel Baca respectively. As related well ahead, also by reasoned supposition, all three of them had been taken away from Zuñi as little girls by Diego de Trujillo in 1662, finally to be adopted as part of her own family by Doña Bernardina de Salas y Trujillo. Subsequently, the three were generally considered to be the real sisters of the Hurtado wife of Don Fernando Durán y Chaves while bearing their own distinctive surnames. Nor should all this deter our Doña Juana Montoya de Ynojos from having been the wonderful mother of the ten children she bore to Pedro Durán y Chaves. The best testament to her maternal influence, and her genes, is her progeny. And so we take up again her seven daughters and three sons in the three age groupings as outlined in her husband's last will.

3. The Four Eldest Daughters

1. *Manuela Chaves* had married a Sebastián Marcelino Niño Ladrón de Guevara, who was the will's executor as we recall. But we have no record of the marriage, or any other particulars except the baptism of a son in Albuquerque, christened Lugardo on February 20, 1730. As for the father's origin, he could have been the son of any one of three related individuals at El Paso del Norte named Pedro Ladrón de Guevara, Miguel Ladrón de Guevara, and Cristóbal Marcelino, this one recorded in 1717 as a native of Osuna in Andalucía, and bearing the additional name, Ladrónde Guevara. For Sebastián, after his Chaves wife died, moved back there and remarried in 1740. If the boy Lugardo and any other children of theirs were alive, he must have taken them along, for this particular surname disappeared from New Mexico at this very time. It was being used in Santa Fe by a prominent Ortiz fellow, but this was a harking back to a different paternal ancestor of his in Mexico City. (Incidentally, this justly proud Don Nicolás Ortiz, himself a native of Mexico City, married a Juana Baca of Bernalillo in 1702, thereby providing his many descendants with touches of Analco and Cíbola.)

---

2. *Mónica Chaves* was sixteen when, as Doña Mónica de Chaves, daughter of Pedro de Chaves and Juana Montoya, she married Antonio Baca, eighteen, of Bernalillo on June 16, 1726. His parents were listed as "unknown," a common practice when it came to the illegitimates of the higher-class families, whereas in those of the humbler ones at least the mother was named. Moreover, the pair was related to each other. Antonio was actually the son of Josefa Baca, an unmarried daughter of that Manuel Baca who had started the new town of Bernalillo on his

property; she had her own prosperous place at Pajarito where she brought up her six natural children which she named in her will of 1746, this Antonio being the eldest. He and Mónica had at least eight children of their own at Pajarito; years later they apparently moved up to Santa Fe where most of the children got married. These Baca individuals were Juan Antonio, Barbara Antonia, Pedro Antonio, Josefa Apolonia, Diego Antonio, Juan Domingo, José Antonio, and María Ignacia.

1) *Juan Antonio Baca*, the eldest, married Maria Romero in Santa Fe on September 17, 1753, she being the daughter of Antonio Romero and Nicolasa del Castillo (who as a widow had later married a Miguel Ortiz of Santa Fe in 1737). They had at least ten children, the eldest of whom, Luis María Baca, will be soon treated more at length for a signal thing he did at the Caja del Rio property he inherited from his Castillo grandmother. 2) *Barbara Antonia Baca* first married José Pablo Rael de Aguilar of Santa Fe, a nephew of that Eusebio Rael de Aguilar who had tried to marry Mónica's aunt Doña Isabel de Chaves back in 1718, and then, on July 6, 1742, she married a European Spaniard named Juan Bautista Durán Bachicha. 3) *Pedro Antonio Baca*, born September 25, 1733, might have died young since he is not heard of again. 4) *Josefa Apolonia Baca*, born March 29, 1736, married Clemente Gutiérrez, a fellow from Aragón in Spain, on October 13, 1755. 5) *Diego Antonio Baca*, born June 3, 1738, married Juana Sáenz Garvisu, daughter of another Spaniard from Spain, Manuel Sáenz Garvisu and his wife María Ignacia Lucero de Godoy. 6) *Juan Domingo Baca*, born November 3, 1741, first married María de Loreto Garvisu, sister of his brother's wife just mentioned and by whom he had five children, and then Gertrudis Ortiz by whom he had eleven more. 7) *José Antonio Baca,* born February 23, 1744, might also have died young. 8) *María Ignacia Baca*, born April 23, 1746, married Francisco Trebol Navarro, also a new arrival in New Mexico but whose origin is unknown.

Here we can see how so many of the Baca children of Mónica Chaves got European connections to make their own children quickly "restored" *españoles.* But one of her Baca grandsons deserves special attention for different reasons. He was *Luis María Baca*, the eldest son of Mónica's eldest son Juan Antonio Baca and María Romero. By the turn of the century he had established his domain at La Caja del Río, near the new settlement of Peña Blanca, and which he had inherited from his Castillo grandmother and her second Ortiz husband. (The place was called Santa Cruz, which now lies beneath the waters of Cochiti Dam near the intake tower.) Here he decided to restore the plain Baca name to the original *Cabeza de Baca (Vaca)*, thus starting a distinct New Mexico family bearing the full appellation. Somehow he had come to hear the story of the famed Álvar Núñez Cabeza de Vaca who, long before New Mexico was first settled, had traversed the continent from Florida as far as these parts before turning southward to New Spain, after which he composed a marvelous account of his adventures. Luis María, presuming that he had to be his direct ancestor, used this excuse for adopting his full name.

He had very many children by three successive wives between 1777 and 1810, some of whom retained the plain Baca name while others flaunted their father's newly discovered family identification. From among the latter, two of his grandsons stand out following the arrival of Bishop Lamy in 1851 with his aide Father Machebeuf. *One of them was Francisco Tomás C. de Baca who, with his clever syntax, needled Lamy with the breaches of the confessional secret by Machebeuf; his younger brother, Padre José de Jesús C. de Baca, disgusted by Machebeuf's foul persecution of the native clergy, moved down to the Las Cruces area where he was greatly admired, and then further down into Mexico when the Gadsden Purchase placed that same area under Lamy's jurisdiction.*[1]*—A later proud descendant of Luis María was Ezequiel C. de Baca who was elected New Mexico's second State Governor in 1916, but unfortunately died after his first few weeks in office.*

However, as is usually the case with other such outstanding families, these people, while glorying in what they considered their pure Spanish ancestry and historic surname, had forgotten that their petite dynasty had very much depended on a female named Chaves for its start, while also inheriting some remote Analco and Cíbola genes on both the Baca and Chaves lines.

---

3. *Josefa Chaves*, as we also know from her father Pedro's last will, was the wife of a Francisco Sánchez. He was a son of Jacinto Sánchez de Yñigo and his second wife named María de Castro Xabalera. This brings up another sally into vague ancestral origins similar to that of her own Ynojos mother. The name Sánchez de

1. The case was fully treated in *But Time and Chance*, my biography of the famed Padre Martínez of Taos.

Yñigo first appears among the New Mexico refugees at El Paso del Norte following the Pueblo Revolt of 1680, in a family consisting of an unmarried woman by the name of Juana López with one daughter and two sons. The first one, calling herself "Doña" Francisca Sánchez de Iñigo (but giving no parents for reasons previously cited), married Juan García de Noriega at El Paso del Norte on May 4, 1681, he being the son of that brave *teniente* Alonso García who had saved the Río Abajo refugees the year before by bringing them safely down to El Paso del Norte.

Going back to the three children of Juana López, Pedro Sánchez de Iñigo, born in New Mexico around 1673, came to marry Leonor Baca, a first cousin of that Manuel Baca of Bernalillo. This was at San Lorenzo del Paso in 1691, when, unlike his sister Francisca, he was not ashamed to say that he was the natural son of Juana López; and once he was referred to there as Pedro López de Yñiguez. His Baca wife, after their return to New Mexico, was later killed during that minor 1696 Pueblo Revolt north of Santa Fe, after which he married a María Luján of Santa Fe in 1698, when he again declared that Juana López was his natural mother.

The other brother, Jacinto Sánchez de Yñigo, said that he was born in the Río Abajo (around 1664) and had married an Isabel Telles Jirón at El Paso del Norte; following her death in Santa Fe in 1696, he then married María de Castro Xabalera, a native of Sombrerete from among the Zacatecas colonists who had arrived the previous year, when he, like his sister Francisca, referred to himself as the son of "parents unknown." But in 1692 at El Paso del Norte, he and Juana López herself had stood as witnesses for a wedding. Hense there is no doubt that he and his elder sister Francisca were also the natural children, as was Pedro, of Juana López.

Among this Jacinto's children by his first Telles Jirón wife was José Sánchez, married to Teresa Jaramillo, who produced a junior Jacinto Sánchez who became the husband of Efigenia Chaves; another son by his second Castro wife, Francisco Sánchez, is the one who married Efigenia's older sister, this our Doña Josefa Chaves.

But how did our Josefa's husband get his unusual surname, we are curious to know; and who was Juana López, its originator? My studied guess is that the *Yñigo* part of the name (as the origin of the *Yñiguez* patronym also used by the Ynojos people previously treated), had been adopted by Juana López to designate her three illegitimate children as people of substance. Yet, who was Juana López herself? She, whether an *española* or *mestiza*, had to be a strong and very independent woman who, like some females in every age, and some of them today, preferred to do without bothersome husbands, content to be the kept mistress of some fellow they liked. Everybody knew it and took it for granted. And she seems to be a Juana López del Castillo whose family, next to that of Pedro López del Castillo (her brother?), were remembered among the twelve founding families of Albuquerque, this being the general area where she had lived prior to 1680, based on the testimony of one of her sons as being a native of the Río Abajo.

Hence her own surname came from one of two brothers, Diego and Matías López del Castillo, natives as they put it of the "Realms of Castile," who had come to New Mexico sometime before 1630. The second brother, Matías, married to Ana Pérez de Bustillo (aunt of Miguel de Ynojos or Iñiguez), was apparently the grandfather of Pedro and Juana López del Castillo who were among the first settlers of Albuquerque. And so this Juana López had had her three natural children during the decade preceeding the 1680 Pueblo Revolt by some fellow using "Sanchez" somewhere in his multiple surname, and which she combined with her rendering of the Yñiguez one. Moreover, in a family recollection of 1770, the Sánchez de Yñigo progeny were accused of being "Indian," hence Juana's lover could have been from among the Analco *mestizos*, and who had died prior to the Pueblo Revolt. As said before, this has been a long guess, but still a most important one because many of these particular Sánchez people would continue intermingling with those of the Chaves clan.

Our Josefa Chaves and her Francisco Sánchez had six children whom we know about from their respective marriages: Juan Cristóbal, María Bárbara, Diego Antonio, Marcos, Joaquín, and Teresa, two of whom had outstanding descendants:

1) *Juan Cristóbal Sanchez*, born September 21, 1726, married a Juana Chaves (her parents unidentified so far) on September 24, 1758. Any children of theirs are unidentifiable to date. 2) *María Bárbara Sánchez*, born December 26, 1730, as Doña Bárbara Sánchez, thirty-one, daughter of the *capitán* Don Francisco Sánchez, deceased, and Doña Josefa Durán y Chaves; she was asked for in marriage by Don Joaquín José Pino in 1763, he being thirty-seven and a native of Mexico City, the son of Don Juan Bautista Pino and Doña Teresa de Ávila y Calle, both

deceased. Here a dispensation in the second degree of affinity was requested because the bride, as a destitute orphan (!), had had previous carnal relations with the groom's brother (Mateo José Pino). This must have taken quite a bit of mulling to resolve by the authorities, for the wedding did not take place until August 28, 1764. (These two Pino brothers had come from Mexico City with their merchant father prior to 1747, setting up their mercantile headquarters at El Rancho de San Clemente, present Los Lunas.) Bárbara's Pino husband died four years after their marriage, leaving her with a little girl named Catarina Pino, who first married an Antonio Luna who was later killed by the Apaches prior to 1782, probably around 1770. From this pair was to descend a prominent Luna family of the last century which, for its having a more immediate descent from another and closer Chaves grandmother, will be treated later on. Here I point out a humbler personal line.[2] After the death of her Luna husband at the hands of the Apaches, Catarina Pino married a soldier of Santa Fe, Cleto Miera y Pacheco, who was the son of *Bernardo Miera y Pacheco, a native of El Valle de Carriedo in Spain, who in New Mexico became a famous explorer of 1776 and is better known as a cartographer for his regional maps which are much prized today.* (See map heading this section and my translation of the *The Dominguez-Escalante Journal, 1776.*)

3) *Diego Antonio Sánchez*, the second son of Josefa Chaves, married Ana María Álvarez del Castillo on April 6, 1756, she being the eldest daughter of another newcomer, Juan Miguel Álvarez del Castillo, origin not known, by his first wife Barbara Baca. Others of this Castillo's children by three successive wives would be intermarrying with those of several Chaves families. 4) *Marcos Sánchez*, as an *español* of Tomé, twenty-two, married Doña Margarita Valdés of Abiquiú north of Santa Fe, the daughter of Don Juan Valdés and Doña Teresa Martínez, in 1763. She was obviously descended from José Luis Valdés of Oviedo in Spain, one of the soldiers recruited by Governor Vargas in 1692. 5) *Joaquín Sanchez* in 1769, as an *español* of Tomé, twenty-three, the son of Don Francisco Sánchez and Doña Josefa Durán y Chaves, married Doña Ana María Padilla, thirteen of Los Padillas, daughter of Don Diego Padilla and Doña Barbara Yturrieta. 6) *Teresa Sánchez* became the wife of Mateo José Pino, brother of the above Joaquín Pino who had married her sister Bárbara (and with whom he had been intimate). A son of theirs, *Pedro Bautista Pino, would be the first and only Delegate to the Spanish Cortes*

2. *GENEALOGY:* **Josefa D. y Chaves, Bárbara Sánchez, Catarina Pino, José Enrique Luna, Toribie Luna, María Encarnación Luna, Eugenio Chávez, Fabián Chávez, Fr. A. Chávez.**

at Cádiz in 1812, and where he proudly stated that New Mexico's Hispanic people were all pure Spaniards, untainted by either Indian or African blood. He was naturally ignorant of the fact that his Pino grandparents had been restored *españoles* of Mexico City (unless both had come from Spain), while his Sánchez mother in both her own parents' lines had some distant genes from Cíbola and Santa Fe's Analco from much further back.

---

4. *Efigenia Chaves*, the last of the married daughters mentioned in her father Pedro's will, was married to Jacinto Sánchez II, who was a nephew of her sister Josefa's husband. Two of their known children were: 1) *Pedro Sánchez* who in 1761 as Don Pedro Sánchez of Atrisco, twenty-seven, the son of the *capitán* Don Jacinto Sánchez and Doña Efigenia Durán y Chaves, married Doña María Luz Baca, daughter of the *capitán* Don Manuel Baca and Feliciana Durán y Chaves, both having been dispensed as second cousins because of " the paucity in this Kingdom of blood quality." (The same excuse was being given for several such close marriages at this period.) 2) *Juan Domingo Sánchez* who in 1763, as plain Domingo Sánchez, *español* and thirty, the son of Jacinto Sánchez and Doña Efigenia Durán y Chaves, married María Rosalía Baca, *española* of El Río Turbio (today Río Puerco), daughter of the *capitán* Marcos Baca and María Jaramillo, they being second and third cousins in one line and second cousins in another, and so proven by very complicated ancestral lines without names being given—clear to those involved at the time but so difficult for us to finally make out.

Efigenia and Jacinto also had their servants bearing their masters' name. In 1769 there was the marriage of Isidro Sánchez, eighty-one, a *genízaro* of Atrisco who was an *indio criado* of Efigenia Chaves, with an *india criada* of Don Pedro Otero of Atrisco (this man Efigenia's reputed half-brother as we shall see later). Also, in 1774, there was the marriage of an Antonio José Chaves, twenty, an *indio criado* in the house of Pedro Chaves (Efigenia's father), with Antonia Sánchez, seventeen, a *coyota* reared in the house of Jacinto Sánchez, deceased.

So much for the story of the four adult and married daughters of Pedro Durán y Chaves and Juana Montoya de Ynojos. Now we come to the second group of three in Pedro's last will.

4. Eldest Son and Two Sisters

5. Francisco Xavier Chaves, the first of the three grown-up children with his sisters Quiteria and Juana, was not quite the wastrel that his four older sisters made him out to be, when we consider the prosperous family that he reared; or else, as it happens when several girls precede a boy, they had been unable to understand his male proclivities so different from their own. He married Manuela Padilla on September 29, 1735, some six or seven months after his father's estate was probated and less than two months following his death. He is further identified in an 1838 family tree as the son of Pedro Durán y Chaves. His wife was a daughter of Diego Padilla and María Vásquez Baca (grand-daughter of Bernalillo's founder), most of whose seven Padilla children came to marry a Chaves. She and her Francisco Xavier had the following known children: Tomás, Domingo, María Teresa, María Concepción, José Antonio, and Miguel Antonio, some of whom married as follows:

1) *Tomás Chaves*, born December 20, 1737, married María Josefa Padilla, his second cousin as well as sister-in-law, on October 20, 1759, and both were still living at his ranch of Los Padillas in 1790. Three known children of theirs were: a) María Úrsula Chaves who in 1797, as Doña María Úrsula Chaves of Los Padillas, daughter of Don Tomás Durán y Chaves and Doña María Josefa Padilla, married Manuel de Arteaga, a widower and native of Mexico City; b) Gerónimo Chaves who in 1798 as plain Gerónimo Chaves, twenty-five, the son of plain Tomás Chaves and Josefa Padilla, married María Barbara Vallejo, *española* of Valencia, fifteen, the daughter of Juan Vallejo, deceased, and Barbara Luna; c) *Francisco Xavier Chaves* (named after his grandfather), who in 1799 married Ana María Álvarez del Castillo, and whose particular high accomplishments require special treatment further on.

2) *Domingo Chaves* in 1764, as Juan Domingo Durán y Chaves, twenty-two and an *español*, the son of Don Francisco Durán y Chaves, deceased, and Doña Manuela Padilla, married Doña Agustina Padilla, his second and third cousin, she being the orphan daughter of Don Francisco Padilla and Doña Isabel Baca, both *españoles* and deceased. He next married, as an *español* still, another second cousin, María Manuela Aguirre, *española*, in 1779, she being the daughter of Don José Calixto Aguirre (origin not known) and Doña María Magdalena Durán y Chaves, both deceased. The latter had been married at Isleta in 1752,

with Bernardo (Hernando) Chaves and María Quintana as their witnesses. 3) *María Teresa Chaves*, who was born in 1749, in 1763 as Doña Teresa de Jesús Durán y Chaves, *española* and thirteen, daughter of Don Francisco Durán y Chaves, deceased, and Doña Manuela Padilla, married her second and third cousin Don Manuel Lucero of Tomé, *español* and twenty-two, son of the *alcalde mayor* Don Miguel Lucero and Doña Rosa Baca, deceased. After Teresa died, Lucero then married a widow of Atrisco, Barbara Montoya, in 1781, she being a close cousin of himself and his former wife as the daughter of Miguel Montoya and Lucía Durán y Chaves. 4) *María Concepión Chaves*, listed in 1768 as Doña María Concepción Durán y Chaves, fourteen, daughter of Don Francisco Durán y Chaves, deceased, and Doña Manuela Padilla; she married Don Antonio Varela, twenty-two, son of Pedro Varela and Casilda Gonzáles, deceased. Of the last two sons listed, *José Antonio Chaves* was born on April 10, 1746, and *Miguel Antonio Chaves* on September 3, 1756; but their own further identification and their marriages, if they every reached adulthood, require futher study.

Now to that one particular son of Tomás Chaves and María Josefa Padilla who, as mentioned before, deserves special treatment. On September 14, 1799, *Francisco Xavier Chaves, español* and thirty, the son of Don Tomás Chaves and Doña Josefa Padilla, married Ana María Álvarez del Castillo, *española* and fifteen, daughter of Don Joaquín Álvarez del Castillo, and Doña Ana María Vallejo. *He is here singled out because on July 5, 1822, he was named the first Governor of New Mexico under the new Republic of Mexico which had won its independence from Spain the year before, and his subsequent career proved to be a most honorable one, the details of which may be found in the history books.* — He and his wife had four or five boys and six girls, several of whom also stand out in local history. The sons were: Tomás, Mariano José, Antonio Nemesio, José, and Antonio José (unless two of this name were one and the same), while the names of the six daughters were Juana, María Francisca, María Merced, María Dolores, Bárbara, and Manuela Antonia. Now to the sons:

1) *Tomás Chaves* had been sent to Durango for his education, and it is said that there he married a niece of Bishop Zubiría, subsequently becoming a lawyer in that city. 2) *Mariano José Chaves*, born on December 8, 1809, is the *Mariano Chaves who served honorably under Governor Manuel Armijo in 1837 and sup-*

plied for him as interim governor during the latter's illness at a critical time. His wife was Dolores Perea, the daughter of Pedro José Perea; a son of theirs, *Jose Francisco Chaves*, born at Los Padillas on June 27, 1833, began his studies at the University of St. Louis until 1846 when the United States annexed New Mexico, and his parents called him back home. *Subsequently he served as a major, then as a lieutenant colonel, in Navajo campaigns and during the Civil War, and also as a Delegate in Congress later on.* 3) *Antonio Nemesio Chaves*, born on Nov. 2, 1815, married María Barbara Olaya Armijo in 1838. 4) *José Chaves* married a Manuela Armijo on April 30, 1830. 5) *Antonio José Chaves* (if not the above Antonio Nemesio) was married to a Bárbara Armijo when, as a travelling merchant, he was murdered by outlaws while crossing the plains near Chaves Creek in Kansas (hence the place's name).

The marriages of five of the daughters to prominent gentlemen of those times may also be found in the history books and other articles. But that of the sixth one, *Manuela Antonia Chaves*, merits particular attention here. The widow of young José María Gutiérrez of Bernalillo, *she was the first native woman of New Mexico to join the Sisters of Charity in Santa Fe, with whom she lived as a greatly revered "Sister Dolores" until her death on April 13, 1887*. Old Don Fernando Durán y Chaves of a hundred and more years back would have beamed with pride had he been able to foresee a family like this one, even if it was directly descended from his not too promising second son Pedro.

And here another interesting item can be brought in by way of contrast with that of the holy nun of Santa Fe, and in the same time period. In 1879 there lived in Santa Fe a lady named Mercedes Chaves, who might have belonged to this Chaves group or else a closely related branch of the same social standing. (Or was she the nun's elder sister, María Merced, mentioned previously?) She was the wife of Jean-Baptiste Lamy, a nephew and namesake of the famed first Archbishop of Santa Fe who was still living. Insanely jealous of the attentions being paid his wife, this Lamy shot and killed the cathedral architect, another Frenchman named François Mallet, in early September of that year; whereupon Doña Mercedes Chaves de Lamy, following a universal Spanish female custom when faced with any serious embarrassment, dramatically took a poison which she had made sure was not fatal.

---

6. *Quiteria Chaves*, who followed her brother Francisco Xavier, was already approaching womanhood when her father Pedro married a second time in 1728. She could well have had her troubles with her young stepmother Gertrudis Sánchez, if not also being influenced by the latter's example which, as we shall see, was none of the best. For she began having children out of wedlock as we learn from a 1764 land dispute which was initiated by her son Pedro Durán y Chaves in the name of his Chaves brothers. The suit was against some sons of a Bernardo Padilla whom she had eventually married, hence these were evidently half-brothers of the plaintiff. This Bernardo was the son of that Diego Padilla frequently mentioned before and María Vásquez Baca, hence we see further relationships here also. What we know for sure is that Quiteria and Bernardo had a son who at Isleta in 1775 as Francisco Padilla, *español*, the son of Don Bernardo Padilla and Doña Quiteria Chaves, married Josefa Lucero, an *española* of Tomé and seventeen, who was the daughter of Don Miguel Lucero and Doña Rosalía Abeytia—after having been dispensed as second and third cousins. Here it was shown that the groom's grandfather, Don Pedro de Chaves, was a brother of Don Francisco de Chaves, whose daughter Antonia Chaves was the grandmother of the bride.

---

7. *Juana Chaves*, named in tandem with her brother Francisco Xavier and sister Quiteria, is hard to place. But she seems to be the young woman of this name who married a Domingo Baca. She was dead by 1772 when a daughter, as Juana María Andrea Baca, *española* and twenty-five, the child of Domingo Baca and Juana Chaves, deceased, married a Juan García, *español* and twenty, the son of Toribio García and Antonia Teresa Gutiérrez, also deceased. Then in 1784 the full Chaves name was twice used when José Baca, the son of Domingo Baca and Doña Juana Durán y Chaves, both of them deceased, married his second cousin Doña Victoria Ana Durán y Chaves, she being the daughter of Don Tomás Francisco Durán y Chaves and Doña Tomasa Padilla, deceased. All this strongly suggests that Domingo Baca's wife was actually that daughter of Pedro Durán y Chaves named Juana.

Now to the last three little ones in his last will:

5. The Last Three Minors

8. *Diego Antonio Chaves,* twelve years old when his father Pedro died in 1735, was the first of the three minor children mentioned in the will. He was also the second son, after his much older brother Francisco Xavier, just treated at great length with his large progeny. On December 14, 1740, Diego Antonio married *Juana Silva*, the daughter of Antonio de Silva, a native of Querétaro, and his wife Gregoria Ruíz, born in Mexico City, both of whom had come with the Mexico Valley colonists of 1694. He and Juana Silva had five known children, four of whom married into the family of Manuel Segundo Durán de Armijo and Alfonsa Lucero de Godoy who had moved down from Santa Fe to the Atrisco area. Armijo himself was a grandson of José de Armijo and Catarina Durán, a *castizo* couple which had come with their three grown sons in the colony from Zacatecas of 1695. In 1703, his own father, Vicente Ferrer, 21, then married María Magdalena Arzate, (or Apodaca) also 21; she was half-Tewa, her mother having been captured as a girl in 1680 and subsequently rescued by the Vargas forces in 1692 with a boy and girl she had acquired in the meantime through some of her captors.

Incidentally, Governor Vargas himself chose the girl, María Magdalena, as his godchild when the padres baptized all the rescued children, and here we come to another most interesting episode regarding descent, and reminiscent of that one treated a good while back regarding the black Representative of Pohe-yemo. Far back in 1680, the rebel Tano Indians of Galisteo had killed the Spanish males living nearby, but had taken the young women captive. One of these was *Juana de Apodaca (alias Arzate or Maese)* who was the natural daughter of a Catarina Montaño by a transient named Domingo de Arzate. As just said, she was rescued with other females from the Tewa Indians in 1692, along with some children they had acquired in the meantime. Juana herself had a boy and a girl when thus rescued, when Governor Vargas himself stood as godfather for the girl when she was baptized as *María Magdalena*. Following the Vargas Reconquest of 1693, on May 12, 1697, her mother Juana de Apodaca came to marry Vargas' black drummer, Sebastián Rodríguez by name, who was a native of Luanda in Portuguese West Africa, or Angola. Hence her half-Tewa daughter, María Magdalena, had a genuine black African fellow for a step-father when she married Vicente Ferrer Durán de Armijo in Santa Fe sometime prior to 1706.

Hence, as we shall see, certain Chaves people (including myself, Gov. Manuel

Armijo, and certain very prominent Chaves individuals), while not being direct descendants of Vargas' black drummer, do have him for a remote step-father almost three centuries ago!

The known children of Diego Antonio Chaves and Juana Silva are the following: Pedro, Bárbara, María Guadalupe, Antonio, and Pablo, all of whom married as follows. 1) *Pedro Chaves*, who at Albuquerque in 1772 as Don Pedro Durán y Chaves, *español* and twenty-five, the son of Don Diego y Chaves and Doña Juana Silva, married Doña Catarina Baca, *española* of Fuenclara, daughter of Don Ignacio Baca and Doña Margarita Romero, a witness being a Don Miguel Antonio Durán y Chaves, thirty-one. (Because a grandson of this Pedro became famous in his own right, he requires special attention shortly).

2) *Bárbara (Bárbara Casilda Chaves as named elsewhere)* got married in Albuquerque in 1769 as Barbara Durán y Chaves, twenty, daughter of Don Diego Durán y Chaves and (mother's name omitted by oversight). The groom was Vicente Ferrer Durán de Armijo, twenty-three, the son of Manuel Durán de Armijo and Alfonsa Lucero de Godoy. The best known son of this couple was Manuel Armijo who at Sandía in February, 1818, as Manuel Armijo, *español* of Albuquerque, the son of Vicente Armijo and Doña Barbara Chaves, both deceased, married Doña María Trinidad Gabaldón, fifteen, daughter of Don José Manuel Gabaldón and Doña María Dolores Ortiz. *This is the Manuel Armijo who was Governor of New Mexico, first during the Mexican Period in 1837-1839, and then in 1846, the year when General Kearny and his American Army of the West marched into Santa Fe without firing a shot. As for his own conduct in that momentous event, historians have for long expressed different views.*

A sister of this now famous governor, Isidora Armijo, married a Jesús María Chaves, and these were the parents of David Chávez who married María de la Paz Sánchez. She was the daughter of a Desiderio Sánchez and a younger Bárbara Chávez who was a niece of Governor Manuel Armijo.[2] From this union came two outstanding gentlemen of our times, *Senator Dennis Chávez and Judge David Chávez. The Senator made an enviable record in our National Congress from 1930 to 1962, while his brother, who served as a federal judge in Puerto Rico as well as Supreme Court Justice in his native New Mexico, was also a colonel in our Army's judiciary system during World War II.*

2. *Data from Twitchell and others. Church records are missing for this period.*

To continue with the next three children of Diego Antonio Chaves and Juana Silva: 3) *María Guadalupe Chaves* also got married in Albuquerque in 1774 as María Guadalupe Durán y Chaves, *española* and sixteen, the daughter of Diego Antonio Chaves and (mother's name omitted again by the notary, probably because she was long dead, as happened in other such instances). The groom was her brother-in-law José Durán de Armijo, *español* and twenty-five, the son of Salvador Manuel Armijo and Alfonsa Lucero de Godoy.[3] 4) *Antonio Chaves* in this same year, as an *español* of Atrisco and twenty-eight, the son of Don Diego Antonio Durán y Chaves and Doña Juana Silva, married Doña María Antonia Durán de Armijo, also an *española* and fifteen, daughter of Don Manuel Durán de Armijo, deceased, and Doña Alfonsa Lucero de Godoy. 5) *Pablo Chaves* in 1776, as Pablo Durán y Chaves, *español* and twenty-three, the son of Don Diego Antonio Durán y Chaves and Doña Juana Silva, married Doña Manuela Durán de Armijo, the widow of Cristóbal Jaramillo; she was also a daughter of Don Manuel Durán de Armijo, deceased, and Doña Alfonsa Lucero de Godoy.

Also, going back to that Pedro Chaves who in 1772 had married Catarina Baca, we come to a grandson of theirs who left his mark on New Mexico's early American history. This Pedro and his wife were among the pioneer settlers of the western Cebolleta-San Rafael country when the Navajos were a continual menace. Here one of their sons, Julián Chaves, and his wife María Luz García de Noriega, became the parents of *Manuel Antonio Chaves who, as a Lieutenant Colonel during the Civil War between the States, was instrumental in defeating a Confederate army at Apache Canyon near Santa Fe in 1862, thus putting an end to the Confederacy in the West.* Willa Cather described Col. Chaves briefly but quite handsomely in her classic novel, *Death Comes for the Archbishop*, her "life" of Bishop Lamy of Santa Fe—not knowing that the latter had rashly excommunicated Chaves when he stood for his rights over a dispute regarding some land which adjoined the Guadalupe chapel in Santa Fe. In our day, Marc Simmons published a fine biography of him entitled, *The Little Lion of San Rafael*.

This is the man treated in the beginning as having lost the Chaves signet ring

3. GENEALOGY: **Guadalupe D. y Chaves**, María Isabel Armijo, María Rita Torres, José Francisco Chaves, Eugenio Chávez, Fabián Chávez, Fr. A. Chávez.—These multiple Chaves-Armijo pairings also point to the varied ancestry of Senator Dennis Chávez and his brother David.

of five keys which we presume had been passed down from eldest son to eldest son. But how? His great-grandfather Diego Antonio Chaves was only the second son of Pedro Durán y Chaves, quite younger than the eldest one, Francisco Xavier. Had the latter, the "wastrel" his four elder sisters accused him of being, later swapped it with his younger brother for some ready cash or whatever else? This Col. Chaves married Vicenta Labadía, grand-daughter of Dominique Labadie, a native of France who had married a Micaela Padilla in Santa Fe on November 2, 1766.[4] *She and the colonel were the parents of Don Amado Chaves to whom we owe the story of the ring and how it got lost, and also of Don Irineo Chaves who was also an outstanding citizen of his day.*

---

9. *María Luisa Chaves*, ten years old when her father Pedro died in 1735, a mere child when he remarried in 1728, had been reared with her two small brothers Diego Antonio and Eusebio in their uncle Francisco's house as previously noted. At first I had presumed that she was the same girl as *Lucía*, Francisco's own daughter who married a Miguel Montoya in 1734, but this is entirely impossible when we take dates into consideration. As for this María Luisa herself, there is no trace of any marriage, if she lived to see one. Wives of this name appear in the records, but with no other data to identify her with any of them.

---

10. *Eusebio Chaves*. He was the last of the three minors mentioned in their father Pedro's will, being only a year old, more or less, in 1728 when he with his older orphan siblings, Diego Antonio and María Luisa, were placed in the care of their uncle Francisco Chaves. It is here that the three of them reached maturity, and evidently well-trained by their kindly uncle. We have seen how their much older brother Francisco Xavier, an adult when their father died, did quite well, particularly through the accomplishments of two grandsons of his. Then their slightly elder brother, the Diego Antonio just treated, and reared with them by their good uncle, prospered as well, and with a descendant who also made a name for himself. Now this Eusebio, the youngest of the ten, began trying to emulate the other two brothers without waiting, if we may put it so, for a grand-

4. GENEALOGY: **Dominique Labadie**, Josefa Labadía, María Guadalupe Ribera, María Dolores Alarid, Romualdo Roybal, Nicolasa Roybal, Fr. A. Chávez.

son to carry on the tradition.

On August 19, 1752, when he was about twenty-four, Eusebio married a *Vibiana Martín Serrano* of Alameda, the daughter of Andrés Martín Serrano by his second wife Quiteria García de Noriega, her widowed father having moved down from the Río Arriba's Chimayó to Alameda when he married this García woman on August 16, 1734. This Vibiana's Martín Serrano father, widowed a second time, married a María Dolores Gallegos in 1747, and this is brought in because years later, in 1765, she was suing Eusebio Chaves for having beaten up her aged husband who was also his father-in-law. Whatever the reasons for it were, it does look as though the assailant had done a most cowardly deed in assaulting this much older man; and yet, it could well be that Eusebio had lost his temper when the elderly fellow spoke ill of his demented father Pedro, long dead by now and whom his son did not remember, and about the Chaves folk in general.

For it is evident by this time that Eusebio had developed in himself a pathetic regard for what his Chaves ancestors had done in the past. There was an improbable tradition that he himself journeyed all the way to Spain in order to request titles for himself and his two sons in view of his ancestors' great deeds as the early Conquistadores of New Mexico. The actual fact is that he had made this request to New Mexico's own Governor Mendinueta on April 19, 1774, when he asked for the *alcaldía* of Sandía and San Felipe for himself, that of Jémez, Zia and Santa Ana for one son named Blas, and that of Laguna, Ácoma and Zuñi for the other son, Juan Miguel—and all three offices for life because his own father Don Pedro and his grandfather Don Fernando, as well as he himself, had wrought such grand "*conquistas*." Here one might discern a bit of madness which he had inherited from his father who had begotten him in his failing years, since such megalomania was wholly out of step with current conditions.

At this very time, the ancient and empty Kingdom of New Mexico had at long last been reduced to one of the Interior Provinces of New Spain under a top commander far down in Sonora. The kinds of *alcaldías* over several Indian pueblos were now a thing of the past. Governor Mendinueta, of course, turned down that outlandish petition on May 12, 1775. While granting that Eusebio's ancestors had done such great service in times long past, this governor wrote, he had found out through due investigation that Eusebio himself had taken part in only two campaigns, and in both of them had absented himself at the hour of actual danger.

As just said, Eusebio had two grown sons. The first, baptized *Blas de la Can-*

delaria at Alameda on February 6, 1754 (and so named for the feast of Our Lady of Candlemas, February 2, and that of St. Blaise, February 3, on whose feast throats were blessed with candles), married a Catarina Aranda y Tafoya (or Saavedra) sometime prior to 1775. By this time, Blas had been made the *alcalde* of *genízaro* Abiquiú in the Río Arriba country of his mother, and which looks like a sop from Governor Mendinueta to assuage his overly ambitious father. He later acquired lands in the nearby Chama area, and his signature appears as notary for pre-nuptial investigations made at Santa Cruz in 1780 and 1781. Here he and his wife had a son named *Miguel Mariano Chaves, born on August 18, 1783, who in his adulthood and at his own expense built the first church of San José de Chama with the Durango bishop's authorization dated September 11,1844. (This town with its original church, now called Hernández, has been immortalized in a moonlight photograph by Ansel Adams.)*—One son of his, Jesús María Chaves y Lucero, eventually became a lieutenant in the U.S. Territorial Militia and fought the Confederates at the battle of Valverde.

Eusebio's other son, *Juan Miguel Chaves*, was residing in Los Corrales in 1781 when as Juan Miguel Durán y Chaves, twenty-five, the son of Don Eusebio Durán y Chaves and Doña Vibiana Martín Serrano, he married María Gertrudis Gutiérrez, *española* of Bernalillo and sixteen, she being the daughter of Pascual (?) Gutiérrez, and María Dolores Márquez. He had a sister who in 1797, as Doña *Juana Catarina Durán y Chaves*, a native and resident of San Carlos de Alameda, the daughter of Don Eusebio Durán y Chaves and Doña Vibiana Martín, married Don José Luis Contreras, *español* and more than twenty-five, a native and resident of El Paso del Norte. His parents were Don Antonio Valerio Contreras, deceased, and Doña Antonia Márquez. Sometime before, the marriage pair had been dispensed from a second-degree impediment of illicit coitus, the groom evidently having had relations with a first cousin or aunt of the bride.

6. *Tail End of a Brood*

At long last we come to *Gertrudis Sánchez*, the second wife of Pedro Durán y Chaves whom he married in 1728, not too long after his first wife had passed away, and when he himself seems to have been approaching what appears like a premature dotage. According to the 1735 will, the two had produced five children within seven years, one of which had died. The Albuquerque baptismal register shows only two as having been his own legitimate brood: *Salvador Manuel*, June 9, 1731, and *José*, June 1, 1733, hence both can be presumed to be sons of his. But what about the other two living ones? It does look as though Gertrudis, during her husband's final years of impotence, mental as well as physical, had been "playing around" as the saying goes. About the first son we have no knowledge, while the second one named José, having been married twice and produced several children in Bernalillo, was the José Chaves who was killed by Apaches on the trail near El Paso del Norte, December 9, 1772. The third child was a girl whose name we do not have but who was married to an Antonio Gutiérrez.

The fourth one named *Pedro*, referred to years later as a son of old Pedro de Chaves, brings up the question of legitimacy by subsequent actions on his part. On September 2, 1759, this Pedro Durán y Chaves (as such) married María Juliana Alarí of Santa Fe, a daughter of Jean d'Alary, a native of France who in 1741 had married a daughter of Juan Fernández de la Pedrera, that Spain-born soldier previously mentioned who had been recruited by Governor Vargas in 1692.[5] At the baptism of one son, José Lorenzo, on July 8, 1773, the parents were given as Pedro *Chaves* and Juliana Alarí; for that of the next one, Antonio Rafael, they were noted down as Pedro *Otero* and Juliana Alarí, December 3, 1775; and then for the next one, Vicente Antonio, December 25, 1781, they were Pedro *Chaves* (again) and Juliana Alarí. Another known son, José Estanislao, was registered at the baptism of a grandchild, March 1, 1824, as the son of Pedro *Otero* and Juliana Alarí. Besides, in 1769, Pedro himself had been referred to as Pedro *Otero* when he took part as a witness in a suit involving his supposed half-sister Efigenia Chaves and her husband Jacinto Sánchez. In this same year, as we already saw, an *india criada* of this same Pedro Otero of Atrisco had married a *genízaro criado* who belonged to Efigenia Chaves.

From all this evidence one has to conclude that Gertrudis Sánchez had at least one lover named Otero subsequent to the 1733 birth of that legitimate Chaves child. But who this Otero swain was also poses a mystery, since there had been no previous Oteros in all of New Mexico's history thus far. (The name Pedro Bermúdez Otero appears only once in any extant document, but with no clear indication if he was in the region at this time, or ever at all.) There was a Franciscan named Fray Cayetano Otero who had been the pastor of Albuquerque at various

5. GENEALOGY: **Jean d'Alary**, Manuel Alarí, José María Alarí, María Dolores Alarid, Romualdo Roybal, Nicolasa Roybal, Fr. A. Chávez.

periods between 1733 and 1744, and my guess has been that he could have taken the little orphan Pedro under his wing. (Other friars did this, but mainly with Indians.) Upon reaching adulthood, and well after his marriage in 1759—and following further squabbles over the Chaves inheritance with his much older purported half-sisters—Pedro had finally decided to adopt Otero as his surname, but not without some spurts of hesitation as we have seen.

Or was it because he had come to notice that he looked entirely different from all of his supposed Chaves brethren and relatives? Curiously enough, some of his Otero grandsons, like Territorial Governor Miguel Antonio Otero—whose photograph exists—as well as his immediate descendants, show features which are entirely different from those of contemporary Chaves individuals—as in the photograph of Col. Manuel Antonio Chaves—as well as among descendants on both the Chaves and Otero sides to this day. The Chaves males were generally lean in build, with sharp features and always a full head of hair, whether black or reddish, while the Otero men were short and stout with fair pudgy features on a round head tending toward early baldness. In the so-called vanity biographies appended to local histories in the past century, those early Oteros claimed that their immediate Otero ancestor had come directly from Spain, a vain boast to be sure. And yet, did they actually know as a strict family secret that their patriarch had been a certain Spain-born friar?

Perish the thought. But this brings to mind a hilarious story told to me years ago by that grand lady and author, Erna Fergusson. When Alf Landon was campaigning for the Presidency, his New Mexico advisers took pains to instruct him concerning the local voters who were inordinately proud of their Anglo-American and Hispanic past. And so, when the train stopped in Albuquerque, he came out on the platform of the last car, and began his speech by saying how proud he was to address the descendants of the Pilgrim Fathers and the Franciscan Fathers!

As for the Otero's maternal ancestress, Gertrudis Sánchez, there is no use speculating about her own parentage. One wonders if she might have been related to the Sánchez husbands of Josefa and Efigenia Chaves, but there is no hint anywhere suggesting such a possibility. However, if this were the case, how could these two husbands have had the heart to exclude her and her own children from the inheritance? Such things do happen everywhere when worldly goods are in dispute.

* * *

By way of recapitulation, our Don Pedro Durán y Chaves, as one of the founders of Albuquerque in 1706, spent all of his married life there, and there is no evidence about his ever having been the sole owner of a vast Atrisco Grant which spread far westward to the lands of the Laguna Indians. The Atrisco area itself had been owned since 1705 by his father and younger brothers whose own portions they had sold to each other or to their in-laws, and then their children had subdivided their portions among their own heirs.

Then, does the so-called "Atrisco Grant"—today claimed as an inheritance by scores of individuals—refer to the *estancia* of that former Don Pedro Durán y Chaves who had abandoned it much further back, in 1684, when he moved down to New Spain with all of his family, hence leaving no direct heirs to claim it after New Mexico was resettled in 1693?

III. Antonio Durán y Chaves

Magdalena Montaño
Antonia Baca

1. *All About Weddings*

In 1701 at his father's Bernalillo, Antonio gave his age as twenty-one when testifying in a pre-nuptial investigation. But he had to be some three years older, if we recall him as the third child of four little ones when the family escaped death in 1680. Previously mentioned as being in command of a squad at Atrisco in 1705, following the expulsion of the Apaches from the valley in that year, he was joined by his parents and all of his brethren a short time later. His elder brother Pedro then helped form the nucleus of Albuquerque when it became a formal *Villa* in the following year. As Antonio was ailing at the time, his father Don Fernando offered to replace him as military head at Atrisco for the nonce, but we do not know if this proved necessary. Whatever, Antonio was quite healthy in 1712 when he and his younger brother Francisco were arrested with their father during that crazy fray which concerned Juan González whom their father did not deem quite enough an *español* to be their mayor.

By this time Antonio had been married to a *Magdalena Montaño* by whom he had at least two children: María, born in 1707, and Fernando, born in 1708, and about whom we have no further knowledge. (After this the first baptismal book of Albuquerque has some folios missing, already lost before it was bound in its very old leather cover, and so we do not know of any further children.) If the boy Fernando did reach maturity, he could be the man who married an Antonia Sánchez, as we know from the marriage in 1769 of this couple's son, José Antonio Chaves, with a Mónica Varela. As for Magdalena Montaño herself, she was still living in 1712 during that González altercation just mentioned, but had died prior to 1718 when her husband Antonio remarried. Her own ancestry is quite interesting in itself, while also important to know because two of her Montaño sisters came to marry two of her Chaves husband's brothers.

Their father, Juan Antonio Montaño de Sotomayor, was a native of Mexico City who had come to Santa Fe as a convict sometime before 1680. His was apparently a political exile, although something more serious cannot be discounted. Deciding to stay in New Mexico before his term was over, he had married Isabel Jorge de Vera, daughter of Antonio Jorge de Vera and Gertrudis Baca (and sister of that Antonio Jorge who had been Don Fernando's military aide and friend). Montaño was among the refugees at El Paso del Norte in 1681 when he passed muster as a convict thirty years of age, having a complete set of weapons, a wife, and one female servant, (but no children as yet); he was of medium height and had a lisp along with a fair and pimply complexion. His wife Isabel, by the way, was a granddaughter of that bigamous Canary Islander whose story was fully told in the maternal ancestry of Antonio Chaves' own mother, Doña Lucía Hurtado de Salas.

This Montaño family of sons and daughters, subsequently acquired at El Paso del Norte since 1680, had settled in Santa Fe following the Vargas Reconquest of 1693. Since then the father had died and the sons had gotten married, while the widow was left alone with three unmarried daughters. This is what must have prompted Don Fernando's wife Lucía to invite these relatives of hers and live at their estate in Atrisco. For both women had strong ties going back to those soap operas which had started with that bigamous Diego de Vera, while Don Fernando himself could have been in accord, remembering his old partner Antonio Jorge, Isabel's brother, who was long dead. Also dead and gone, to his relief, was her ex-convict Montaño husband, which made matters easier. But he had not foreseen that the three Montaño girls would soon be marrying three of his sons, something he had to bear in silence since they proved to be a conniving lot who were out to get their man at any cost. This we shall see later on.

As we have just seen, Magdalena Montaño, his son Antonio's wife, had died following their brief marriage and, for all we know, might have been different from her two sisters. Then Antonio got married again in 1718, to an *Antonia Baca* belonging to the Manuel Baca family of the new Bernalillo. This marriage is the one hinted at a good while back as having the elements of gravest scandal, as well as having a connection with the churches just being built in Albuquerque and Bernalillo.

Sometime in March of 1718, Antonio Chaves of Atrisco, widower of Doña Magdelena Montano and son of the *capitán* Don Fernando Durán y Chaves and Doña Lucía Hurtado, asked to marry Doña Antonia Baca, age fifteen, of Bernalillo, and of "unknown partentage." But everyone knew that she was a daughter of Juana Baca, the latter an unmarried daughter of that Manuel Baca who had founded the new town of Bernalillo. Hence the need of a dispensation for Antonio to marry his second cousin. But this was not all by any means. A further dispensation was required in the second degree of affinity because the groom had had carnal relations with a close relative of the bride, and who happened to be his own third cousin besides. The excuses that Antonio proffered for this latter *dispensa* were three fold: First, the bride's poverty and the danger of her losing her virtue should her relatives die; second, the paucity of equal racial status "in this miserable kingdom," as he put it; and third, his own charity in trying to help her, over and above the affection he had for her. The padre was naturally angry and shocked by such disclosures, but finally gave in when he imposed the following drastic penances:

Although a member of the most prominent family as well as head of the militia, Antonio Chaves was to labor manually one day a week for the next four months in the erection of the Albuquerque church, while also begging for alms in behalf of the Poor Souls in Purgatory. Not only had he to donate a thousand adobes for this same church and the same amount for the cemetery walls at Bernalillo, but personally make a hundred of them for the churches of both towns while working for one whole week at each place. This, said the padre, was to deter others from becoming involved in similar scandals. And so the wedding finally took place on March 23, 1718, and then the *velación* or blessing with pomp a month later, on April 24 (probably because the adobe penances had not been completed until this date).

* * *

Years later, in 1733, Antonio Chaves would play a minor but very dramatic part in another marital episode, a sinless one this time, and so much like one of Shakespeare's plays in its plot and characters that I published the incident years ago as a "Romeo and Juliet Story of New Mexico" in the University of New Mexico's *Quarterly Review*.

A cousin of his, Antonio Baca, was a prominent figure among the *españoles* of Santa Fe, who most vehemently forbade a young daughter named Francisca from even meeting a young suitor named Salvador Manuel Armijo. For this Armijo belonged to what her father considered a low *castizo* family which had come from Zacatecas. He even threatened to kill the young man with his own sword if he persisted in meeting the girl secretly. Likewise, the royal family of Governor Bustamante which included the Vicar of Santa Fe at the time, Don José de Bustamante, were all on Baca's side and trying by every means to dissuade his daughter "Juliet" from meeting her Armijo "Romeo," but which she kept doing either in the empty dark church or in the thick groves of the little river's *alameda*. And so Baca decided to send her far away to Albuquerque under the watchful care of his sister, named Josefa Baca, never suspecting that she would turn out to be the bawdy "Nurse" who took Juliet's part in her romance. Soon thereafter, this Aunt Josefa contacted her friend, the Franciscan pastor of Albuquerque, who himself unwittingly assumed the rôle of Shakespeare's kind "Friar Lawrence."

Meanwhile, two "friends of Romeo" had arranged for Armijo to go down to Albuquerque and contact the Nurse. But, instead of having to die like Shakespeare's lovers, our Romeo and Juliet were quickly married by the friar, right after the congregation left the church following the festive Mass of San Lorenzo on August 10, 1733. When word of it leaked out, a duel got started in the front churchyard between Antonio Montoya of Santa Fe, a brother-in-law of Juliet, and the *capitán* Antonio Chaves who was the Nurse's close relative. (In addition the latter was an aunt of his wife Antonia Baca whom he had married fifteen years before under less innocent circumstances.) The many festive bystanders stopped the duel in good time, and so there were no further deaths as in Shakespeare's plays. But, as said before, the plot and characters in both dramas are other wise uncannily the same.

2. *Strong Helpmate and her Orphans*

Antonio Durán y Chaves is recorded as having made a business trip or two, either to Mexico City or only as far as El Paso del Norte, one of which would have been in 1735 when he is mentioned as being "away from the Kingdom" at the time his elder brother Pedro was mentally incapacitated and about to die. This is when, as the third living son of Don Fernando, he came into possession of his father's last will made in 1707. He himself was to pass away prematurely three years later, on May 12, 1738. His young widow Antonia Baca would outlast him for more than thirty years, her own death finally occurring on February 15, 1770.

She never remarried, unlike many a young widow of those times, while apparently becoming more attached to her growing sons. This one gathers from the many times when she was invited to be a godmother at baptisms, always having one or the other of her boys as her partner in the ceremonies. She also seems to have had her way when some of them got married, while folks sometimes referred to her sons by her own Baca surname instead of Chaves. For example, there was one son, Tomás Chaves who, while recorded by this name when he got married in 1742, was recalled generations later as Tomás Baca, yet with a true and legitimate ancestry going back to Don Fernando. Another case is that of another son, Juan Antonio Chaves, whom the notary at his pre-nuptial investigation in 1770 recorded as Juan Antonio Baca (but without saying that he was a "natural" son as was the custom for illegitimate children).

However, there was one direct accusation of marital infidelity after Antonia Baca was dead, and which was patently based on pure gossip; it was brought up when the widow of another son, Cristóbal Chaves, was asked for in marriage by a first cousin of his in 1771, and which shall be treated later on. Instances like these, as said before, point to Antonia Baca's strong hold over her growing sons after her mate had died so prematurely. Yet not all of them having thereby acquired what is now called a mother-complex. All of which brings us to the number of children which she and Antonio Chaves had produced during their twenty or so years of marriage. Since no wills by either of them are extant, we have to depend on scattered sources for their names at least, and without sufficient clues to identify them all as persons. In all, there seem to have been seven sons and three daughters, here listed without any age sequence: Tomás, Miguel, Cristóbal, José Anastasio, Santiago, Francisco, Juan Antonio, Feliciana, Lucía Ana, and María.

Of these three girls, *Feliciana Chaves* did marry a close relative, Manuel Baca, on February 22, 1746, he being supposedly the youngest of the four sons whom her unmarried grand-aunt Josefa Baca had at her ranch in Pajarito—the Nurse in Romeo and Juliet. Both were living at Laguna in 1765 where he was the *alcalde mayor* of the pueblo and district. Their known children are the following: 1) *Antonio Vicente Baca*, born March 28, 1728, who married a María Gertrudis Sánchez on May 31, 1775; 2) *Narcisa Baca*, born November 29, 1750; 3) *María Luz Baca* who as Doña María de la Luz Baca, sixteen, daughter of the *capitán* Don Manuel Baca and Doña Feliciana Durán y Chaves, in 1761 married Don Pedro Sánchez of Atrisco, twenty-seven, the son of the *capitán* Don Jacinto Sánchez and Doña Efigenia Durán y Chaves—and dispensed for being second closed (*cerrados*) cousins because of "the paucity in this Kingdom of blood equality." 4) *María Josefa Baca* who, being sixteen years of age and a native of Atrisco living in Albuquerque, the daughter of plain Manuel Baca and Feliciana Chaves, in 1787 married José Silva, twenty-eight and a native of Zacatecas, the son of Francisco Silva and María Gertrudis Cifuentes; 5) *Antonia Baca* who in 1770 married an Antonio Sedillo.

As for Feliciana's two sisters, *Lucía Ana Chaves* became the wife of a Felipe Romero, and *María Chaves* (it is so sad to read about it when such thing happen) drowned in the Rio Grande when she was only eleven years old. Now to the seven sons of Antonio Durán y Chaves and Antonia Baca.

1.) *Tomás Chaves*, who acted as a sponsor with his mother and also with his sister Feliciana, married a namesake, Tomasa Padilla, and shall be treated more at length below chiefly because of a noteworthy descendant he had. 2.) *Miguel Chaves*, mentioned as a brother of Cristóbal and who acted as a sponsor with his mother, married a Gertrudis de Santistéban of Santa Fe in 1754, and was evidently not related to her in any way. 3.) *Cristóbal Chaves* married María Josefa Núñez in 1756, this bride being a total outsider, and whose marriage merits special treatment later on, as well as with regard to certain of their descendants. 4.) *José Anastasio Chaves* did wed a close relative, Juana María Baca, on October 15, 1758, she being the daughter of Diego Domingo Baca, and possibly a granddaughter of that Josefa Baca of Pajarito, hence some multiple relationships here; we know further about the groom's identity from the 1798 marriage of a daughter, María Soledad, in which he was shown to be the son of Antonio Chaves, the latter a brother of Nicolás Chaves. 5.) *Santiago Chaves*, born in 1733, also married an outsider in 1761 at El Paso del Norte, María Luisa Páez, who was the daughter of Ramón Páez and Manuela Velarde and whom he brought back home. 6.) *Francisco Chaves* appeared once as sponsor with his mother, but as yet cannot be further identified among other males having the same name. 7.) *Juan Antonio Chaves* whom the notary recorded as Baca prior to his marriage in 1770 to Bárbara Montoya.

What follows consists of those fuller details promised about two of the sons, Tomás and Cristóbal.

3. *Some Particular Descendants*

The above-mentioned *Tomás Chaves*, perhaps the eldest of the family, had married Tomasa Padilla on December 3, 1742, she being his second cousin once removed because her grandmother was a sister of his own mother. He is most likely the Don Tomás Chaves who frequently appeared as a pre-nuptial witness between the years 1769 and 1784. He and his namesake wife Tomasa had at least seven children between 1743 and 1767, from among which two of the sons stand out for totally different reasons.

First, *Juan José Chaves*, born on February 4, 1745. In 1772, as an *español* of Atrisco, the son of Don Tomás Durán y Chaves and Doña Tomasa Padilla, deceased, he asked to marry Ana María Baca, *española* of Pajarito forty years old, and twice his third cousin on both the Chaves and Baca sides. Here the respective friars of Albuquerque and Isleta had an argument both as to the degrees of relationship and the disparate ages of the couple, since he was twenty-seven while she was forty. To cap this story, one of the padres ruefully referred to the younger groom as "*nuestro José*," our Joseph, as if pitying the fellow for making such a rash choice, and to the bride as "*vieja y féa*," old and ugly, as though she were a conniving old maid! Items such as this one provide a welcome break in otherwise drab research.

Second, *Francisco Antonio Chaves* has a much better reason for being singled out. He was already a widower in September of 1797 when he married Rosalía Velarde, daughter of José Manuel Velarde and Doña María Manuela Perea, *españoles* of Bernalillo. Afterward they moved north to Abiquiú. Two of their sons born there became noteworthy and, again, in different ways. The first one, *José María Chaves, having served as a young lieutenant toward the end of the Spanish Colonial Period, and then as a colonel during the Mexican one, became a Brevet General in the United States forces during the Civil War, and as a gesture of esteem received from one of his superiors the sword of General Santa Ana of the Mexican War.*

He had married a hometown girl, María de Jesús Martín Serrano, who was a sister of the short-lived wife of the famous Padre Antonio José Martínez of Taos. (The latter studied for the priesthood after his young wife died, and became a noted cleric and politician of his day, the details of which are brought out in my biography of him, *But Time and Chance.*) General Chaves lived to be more than a hundred in the full use of his mental faculties, and he passed away at his native Abiquiú on November 22, 1902; as the obituary put it, he died at the age of one hundred and one years, one month, and twenty-seven days. He is also the man who inherited the 1707 will of Don Fernando Durán y Chaves as a direct descendant of his own grandfather, referred to as Tomás Baca, yet the legitimate son of Antonio Chaves and Antonia Baca.

The general's brother, *Julián Antonio Chaves*, born in Abiquiú on January 7, 1808, the son of Don Francisco Antonio Chaves and Doña Francisca Rosalía Velarde, *españoles*, had driven flocks of sheep to sell in California and decided to stay in Los Angeles; there he acquired property and served in the town's government. *But what he is known for, and only posthumously many generations later, comes from the fact that his property on a hill close to the modern city's civic center is still known as Chávez Ravine, the home of the Los Angeles Dodgers.*

Another son of Antonio Chaves and Antonia Baca, *Cristóbal Chaves*, is important to me and my family, besides many others who can trace their ancestry to him, yet also because some of his grandchildren were to be pioneer settlers well away from the Rio Grande valley, both into what was known as Navajo country and further still to the northeast territory which up to this time had been the realm of the Comanches. While I have several ancestral lines going back to some of the other sons and daughters of Don Fernando, Cristóbal is the one from whom my surname comes.

On June 30, 1756, he married María Josefa Núñez, only fourteen years old and a native of Mexico City, their marriage blessing taking place at the pueblo of Laguna—both such features being out of the ordinary. Previously I had presumed that Cristóbal himself had brought the girl from her distant birthplace, but it is altogether more likely that he found her while on a trip to El Paso del Norte where her parents or other relatives had brought her from the great Capital of New Spain. There they underwent a simple wedding, and when he brought her back home to Atrisco his officious mother could have well disapproved of it for her being an outsider and not from her own closely intermarrying relatives. This one gathers from the strange fact that Cristóbal took her to Laguna Pueblo where his elder sister Feliciana lived with her husband Manuel Baca, who was the local *alcalde* at the time; and there the entry of their *velación* or solemn wedding stands out clearly among the plain Indian entries as that of Cristóbal Chaves, *español*, with María Josefa Núñez, *española* of Mexico City.

Cristóbal himself must have died a decade or so later, prior to 1771 when his widow was asked for in marriage by his first cousin named Bernardo Chaves, a son of Nicolás Chaves and Juana Montaño who will be treated later on. This Bernardo was a very odd old fellow who at first had been married to a Plains Indian servant, as we shall also see anon. Now he contended that no dispensation was required because Josefa's first husband was not really a Chaves, for his being an adulterous son of Antonia Baca by a certain Eusebio Rael de Aguilar (the young swain of 1718 who had tried to marry Don Fernando's eldest daughter Isabel!). The ruse did not work, and years later we find old Josefa Núñez living with the family of her grandson named José Mariano.

This only known son of Cristóbal Chaves and María Josefa Núñez married María Manuela Romero, his second cousin, on February 2, 1773, and they were living at Los Chaves in 1790 with their six children, and with them his long-widowed aged grandmother Doña Josefa Núñez. José Mariano died in Belén in May of 1829, but well before this he and Manuela Romero had more children than the six reported in 1790. All of them are outlined here for a very special reason as pointed out after the last one.

The seven sons were: 1) *José Cristóbal Chaves*, born February 20, 1774, who married Agustina Jurado of Tomé; 2) *Juan José Chaves* who married María Antonia Silva at Belén on April 1, 1810; 3) *José Manuel Chaves*, born at Los Chaves on March 7, 1794, and who married Tomasa González at Cebolleta on August 17, 1817; 4) *José Antonio Chaves* who married María Luz Salaíces (daughter of a Santa Fe soldier from Chihuahua); 5) *José Encarnación Chaves*, born at Los Chaves on March 25, 1796 (feast of the Incarnation), and who married María Rita Torres; 6) *Ambrosio Chaves* who married María Ines Jaramillo at Cebolleta on April 23, 1815; and 7) *José Teodoro Chaves* who married María Josefa Gutiérrez at Cebolleta on April 1, 1818.

The known daughters were: 1) *María Gertrudis Chaves*, born January 11, 1799, who married Juan Antonio Salazar at Cebolleta on November 16, 1814; 2) *María Barbara Chaves* who married Francisco Antonio Romero at Los Chaves on August 20, 1798, and died on May 21, 1831; and 3) *María Nicolasa Chaves* who married José Andrés Jaramillo at Cebolleta on September 4, 1814.

As may be clearly seen from many of these marriages, several sons and daughters were among the pioneer settlers of the western Cebolleta country where the Navajos were a continuous menace in those times. Land had become so scarce in the lower Rio Grande valley, what with so many Chaves folks and others overcrowding the Rio Abajo—and the eldest ones of each family inheriting what was left of the already much-divided property—that the newer generations had to look for land elsewhere. One such new territory, as just said, was the Cebolleta region where the Navajos were continually on the warpath, but this did not deter the settlers at all.

Another such open territory lay in a different direction, toward the still farther northeast where the roving Comanches had held sway for centuries, and whence they had often invaded the Río Arriba Spanish villages and Indian pueblos north of Santa Fe. Thither went several Rio Abajo families seeking new lands for themselves, among them the one of the above-mentioned José Encarnación Chaves who had married María Rita Torres. He had already died when his widow took their entire family to be among the very first settlers of what is now eastern Mora County. There they founded the now long-defunct village of La Ciruela in La Sierra de la Gallina (Turkey Mountain), following the fortunate establishment of Fort Union nearby which made the territory a bit safer from the marauding Comanches. These people and others subsequently founded the town of Santa Clara on the Santa Fe Trail, later called Wagon Mound when the railroad came.[1]

One last item concerning the children of Cristóbal Chaves and María Josefa Núñez with regard to the latter's place of origin. In order to distinguish themselves from the teeming and closely intermarried Chaves population of the Rio Abajo, some of the children of José Mariano at Los Chaves began calling themselves *los Chaves Mexicanos*, since their grandmother had come from Mexico City to break up the long lines of close intermarriages which had existed heretofore. For a short time some even used *Mexicano* for their surname, as may be seen in some church records, particularly those of Cebolleta and San Rafael. I myself, as a lad some seventy years ago, remember hearing my grandfather Eugenio Chávez proudly using the term, for he mistakenly thought that his own grandfather had actually come from Mexico in latter times, and this made him a different Chávez from the countless other such "Smiths" and "Joneses" of Hispanic New Mexico. This also shows how any family remembrance or traditions cannot be trusted unless backed by primary documentary facts.

1. GENEALOGY: **Cristóbal Chaves**, José Mariano Chaves, José Encarnación Chaves, José Francisco Chávez, Eugenio Chávez, Fabián Chávez, Fr. A. Chávez.

* * *

By way of concluding this section, we can say that Antonio Durán y Chaves, the third son of Don Fernando of such glorious memory, had lived in Atrisco ever since he headed its first military post in 1705, and where the two first children by his first Montaño wife were born, as well as where the ten known ones by Antonia Baca had been born and reared. The family holdings had increased in the meantime, for in 1716, after his younger brother Luis had died prematurely, Antonio had bought his portion of the Atrisco lands from the man's widow, and, as we shall see later, his widow Antonia Baca had purchased the portion inherited by Antonio's youngest brother, Pedro Gómez Durán y Chaves.

IV. Francisco Durán y Chaves

Juana Baca

1. A Kindly Uncle and Parent

The fourth son of Don Fernando, and the first to be born during the exile at El Paso del Norte, Francisco was living in Atrisco on May 15, 1713 when, as Francisco Durán y Chaves, more than twenty years old, the son of the *capitán* Don Fernando Durán y Chaves and Doña Lucía Hurtado of Atrisco, he married *Doña Juana Baca*, fourteen, of Bernalillo, who was of "unknown parentage" as well as his second cousin. Of course, everybody knew that she was the natural daughter of Juana Baca *La Vieja* (the Elder) as folks often put it, and who was the sister of Antonia Baca who five years later would become the second wife of his elder brother Antonio. Witnesses to the marriage were the groom's sister Doña María de Chaves Hurtado with her husband Antonio de Ulibarrí. Later on Francisco was being referred to as a *capitán*, hence involved with the local militia like his elder brothers Pedro and Antonio.

Francisco is the kind uncle who took in the three younger children of his brother Pedro when the latter in his dotage entered his second marriage in 1728. By this time he must have had children of his own; yet, because of those missing folios in the first baptismal book of Albuquerque, we have no knowledge of their births. From other sources we know of the existence of these earlier ones: 1) *Agustín Chaves* who died young on January 7, 1741; 2) *Ignacio Chaves* who first married Gregoria Maese and then Úrsula Sánchez in 1770; 3) *María Chaves* who also died young on May 9, 1744; 4) *María Isidora Chaves* who married her namesake Isidro Antonio Maese in 1760; and 5) *Lucía Chaves* who became the wife of Miguel Montoya. Those appearing later in the baptismal records were: 6) *José Vicente Chaves*, born February 14, 1730; 7) *Miguel Antonio Chaves*, born November 26, 1735, who married Francisca Baca on August 29, 1781; 8) *Margarita Chaves*, born January 23, 1734, who married Salvador García in 1761; and 9) *Juana Chaves*, born January 10, 1744. Hence there were apparently nine children in all. (One anonymous daughter had a natural child named María Bárbara Chaves who married her second cousin Juan Vallejo in 1766, and could have been the Juana just listed.)

In the 1760 marriage of his daughter María Isidora, the *capitán* Don Francisco

Durán y Chaves is mentioned as already deceased. Whatever else we know about three of his married daughters is the following:

---

1. *Lucía Chaves*, who married a widower named Miguel Montoya in 1734, is identified as Francisco's daughter from the marriage of their daughter Bárbara Montoya in 1770. This young lady, fourteen, the child of the *capitán* Don Miguel Montoya, deceased, and Doña Lucía Durán y Chaves, was asked for in marriage by Juan Antonio "Baca," thirty-two and an *español* of Atrisco, the son of Antonia Baca (and Antonio Chaves, long dead). So that they could be dispensed as first and second cousins, it was revealed that the groom's mother was the sister of Juana Baca, the mother of Lucía Chaves. This is where we learn that this Lucía was the actual daughter of Francisco Durán y Chaves, and not, as I had once supposed, the "Luisa" of his brother Pedro whom he had adopted when Pedro remarried in 1728.—In 1781, Lucía's daughter Barbara Montoya, widowed of her husband Antonio Baca (Chaves), married another second cousin named Manuel Lucero of Los Padillas. He was the son of Miguel Lucero and Rosa Baca, both of them deceased, and first had been married to a Teresa Chaves, daughter of a younger Francisco Durán y Chaves and his wife Manuela Padilla. Barbara and Manuel Lucero had a daughter, Manuela Lucero, who married a Pablo Baca in 1803.[1]

---

2. *María Isidora Chaves*, when she married in 1760, was identified as Doña María Isidora Durán y Chaves, *española*, daughter of the *capitán* Don Francisco Durán y Chaves, deceased, and Doña Juana Baca, while the groom was simply Isidro Antonio Maese, *español* and fifteen, a soldier of Santa Fe and the son of the *sargento* Bartolomé Maese and Juana Valerio, deceased. At least she did not wed a relative.

---

3. *Margarita Chaves* was identified in 1761 as Doña Margarita Durán y Chaves,

1. GENEALOGY: Lucía D. y Chaves, Barbara Montoya, Manuela Lucero, Tomás Baca, Nicanora Baca, Fabián Chávez, Fr. A. Chávez.

twenty-eight, the daughter of the *capitán* Don Francisco Durán y Chaves, deceased, and Doña Juana Baca. She had been married before to a Juan de Anaya who was killed by the Apaches on the road between Chihuahua and El Paso del Norte. Her present suitor was Salvador García, *español* and forty-nine, the son of the *capitán* Tomás García and Juana Hurtado, both deceased, and himself widowed of Catarina Sánchez who lay buried in the Albuquerque church. The pair had to be dispensed from a multiple relationship of third-degree consanguinity on the maternal side besides the fourth degree of affinity, on grounds that he had several orphans to be cared for, while she had four of them. But what boggles the mind is the way the relationships were described, as were so many others in those times. One witness said that the groom's grandfather was a brother of the mother of the bride's grandmother, while the grandfather of the first Sánchez wife was a second cousin of the bride's grandfather. Another witness said that the first Sánchez wife was the granddaughter of a second cousin of the bride's grandfather, her grandfather and the bride's grandmother being second cousins! For whatever reason, the dispensation, dated July 8, 1761, came from El Paso del Norte.

2. *Some Odd Fellows*

Now to what we know about two of Francisco's sons, Ignacio and Miguel Antonio, and perhaps José Vicente.

1. *Ignacio Chaves* had first been married to a Gregoria Maese by whom he had at least one son and two daughters. In 1766, Juana Chaves of Atrisco and aged fourteen, daughter of Ignacio Chaves and Gregoria Maese, married José Baca, *español* and twenty-five, living at Nuestra Señora del Río Puerco, the son of the *capitán* Marcos Baca and María Jaramillo. Since they were third cousins, a family tree of both parties was provided in this case, and going back to their common ancestor, that Manuel Baca who had founded the new town of Bernalillo. Then in 1775, and widowed of José Baca, this Juana calling herself Juana María Concepción Chaves, *española* of El Sauzal and the daughter of Ignacio Chaves and Gregoria Maese, deceased, married Mariano (?) Sánchez, *español* of Los Chaves, son of Juan Cristóbal Sánchez and another Juana Chaves, after being dispensed as second and third cousins. In this same year of 1775, another daughter, as Doña Josefa Durán y Chaves, *española* and sixteen, daughter of Don Ignacio Durán y

Chaves and Doña Gregoria Maese, deceased, married Pablo Durán de Armijo, *español* and twenty-eight, son of Don Manuel Segundo Durán de Armijo, deceased, and Doña Alfonsa Lucero de Godoy.

Then in 1781, there occurred the marriage of the son, Francisco Antonio Chaves, an *español* of Atrisco, the son of Ignacio Antonio Chaves and Gregoria Maese, deceased, with his second cousin Feliciana Sánchez, *española* of Atrisco, and daughter of Jacinto Sánchez, deceased, and Efigenia Chaves, the bride being the widow of José Hurtado de Mendoza. (This fellow was different from the New Mexico Hurtados, being a native of Jérez de la Frontera in Spain, and who as a widower had married Feliciana in 1766; he was once reprimanded for having examined a girl's proof of virginity much too literally.)

Yet, there was another son of Ignacio, and whose identity we owe to the research of Elizabeth A. H. John of Austin, Texas. *Francisco Xavier Chaves, born around 1760, the son of Ignacio Chaves and Gregoria Maese of Atrisco, around the year 1770 was captured as a boy by the Comanches while herding the family flocks. His captors later sold him to the Taovayas, from whom he escaped in 1784 and found his way to San Antonio de Béjar.* From here in 1785, along with Pedro Vial and others, he volunteered to carry Gov. Cabello's peace overtures to the Comanches, and returned with the latter's delegation for a peace treaty. In 1788 he enlisted in the Béjar Company as soldier-interpreter, and in 1791 got a furlough to visit his New Mexico, whence he returned with affidavits of family descent produced at Isleta on July 12, 1792. He retired as a lieutenant in 1829, and died in San Antonio in 1832. Married twice, he had eleven children by the first wife, Juana Padrón, and five by the second one, Micaela Fragoso.

And now comes a more interesting and revealing view of the children's father Ignacio. In 1768, Don Ignacio Chaves, *español* of Atrisco, the son of Don Francisco Durán y Chaves and Doña Juana Baca, and widowed of Gregoria Maese, asked to marry Doña Ursula Bernardina Sánchez, daughter of Don Jacinto Sánchez and Doña Efigenia Durán y Chaves. (One can see at a glance that she was very closely related, both by blood and by affinity.) The petition for a dispensation from the second and third degrees of consanguinity, and the third of affinity, had been sent to the bishop's court in Durango, but with no reply as late as 1770. In this year, still insisting on this marriage, Ignacio complained before a notary that the dispensation must have been denied simply because he had failed to send the required fee of sixteen *pesos*. Evidently a skinflint, he ignorantly declared that a Church decree forbade the "sale" of such dispensations; besides, said he, it was a well-known fact that Indians and mixed-breeds did not have to pay for them. (Here the fellow misinterpreted the faculty which the Franciscans had of dispensing all Indians as "neophytes," and without charge, but not the *mestizos* who led the life of the Spanish folk.) And so Don Ignacio began proving that he enjoyed the same privileges because he had plenty of Indian blood himself.

He said that his grandmother Juana Baca had some Indian blood on her own father's side, besides being a *mulata* on her mother's. Furthermore, the bride's father, José Sánchez, had Indian blood, while his wife Teresa Jaramillo was Indian on her father's side as well as a *mulata* on her mother's side.

To his embarrassment, if he was capable of such a thing, the awaited dispensation arrived from the Durango chancery right after he had made his penny-pinching harangue. Without doubt he is the Ignacio Durán y Chaves who appears as a pre-nuptial witness between the years 1772 and 1778.

2. *Miguel Antonio Chaves*, *español* of Sauzal, the son of plain Francisco Chaves and Juana Baca, in 1781 asked to marry Francisca Baca, *española*, the daughter of Marcos Baca and María Silva, and they were dispensed from the impediment of consanguinity in the third and fourth degree. But the notary did not think it worthwhile to honor him or his parents with any titles or the full name of Durán y Chaves. Perhaps the groom himself did not care to use them either, and therefore seems to have been altogether different from his brother Ignacio. To all appearances, unless it was a namesake cousin of his, this was the *Miguel Antonio Chaves who founded the brand-new Spanish town of Socorro in 1816, having first made this proposal a couple of years before to the government while accompanied by Pedro Bautista Pino*. For this he led other families from Tomé and Belén to the vacant but still Apache-infested area where the ancient pre-Revolt Piro pueblo of Socorro had stood with its grand Mission of Our Lady of the Assumption. The walls of it were still standing, at least the lower tiers of thick adobe, and upon them the settlers built their own new church, and, as it also happened with other town founders, Chaves gave it the title of San Miguel after his own heavenly namesake.

3. *José Vicente Chaves*. As we have seen, there was a third son of Don Francisco bearing this name who was baptized on February 14, 1730. But now a puzzle arises as to his real identity. Did he die young, or else fails to appear in any of the surviving documents? As shown long before in connection with Josefa de Hinojos,

the good mother-in-law of Pedro Durán y Chaves, there was a bellicose fellow brashly calling himself "Don" José Vicente Durán y Chaves of Atrisco, yet admitting that he was of unknown parentage. This he did when he asked to marry a very young Aragón maiden in 1775, when he likewise brought up the fact that both he and the girl had Zuñi blood from a common ancestress, the same Josefa de Hinojos. This brash revelation of his, and also connected with the problems of marital dispensations, is so much like the 1770 harangue of Ignacio Chaves just treated at length, that this José Vicente appears to have been his brother of this name.

Yet, that problem of self-acknowledged illegitimacy remains. Who was this José Vicente who, although patently an illegitimate, proudly boasted of his full Durán y Chaves surname, and with the "Don" prefix besides? What seems likely is that the ever kindly Don Francisco D. y Chaves had in 1730, right after its birth, adopted the child of a female servant who had been made pregnant by any young Chaves stud of the Atrisco households. Then, when it was baptized, the padre mistakenly recorded the child as Francisco's own son. (This happened in rare instances.) And so young José Vicente grew up learning the unsavory habits of his elder adoptive brother Ignacio. *Quién sabe?*

* * *

From all the foregoing information we can discern that Francisco Durán y Chaves had been a resident of Atrisco ever since 1705 and, moreover, that he had always been an upright person with a generous heart. His wife Juana Baca seems to have shared his fine qualities.

V. Luis Durán y Chaves

Leonor Montaño

1. *A Wayward Young Widow*

In June of 1707 young Luis deposed that he was nineteen years old, the son of the *capitán* Don Fernando Durán y Chaves and Doña Lucía Hurtado, *españoles* of Atrisco, when he asked to marry *Doña Leonor Montaño*, thirteen, daughter of Antonio Montaño, deceased, and Doña Isabel Jorge, likewise *españoles* of Atrisco. As with the subsequent marriage of his elder brother Antonio with hs bride's sister, Magdalena Montaño, a full dispensation for second and third cousins was granted. Moreover, Luis had had previous carnal relations with the girl who had just reached puberty, and the wedding was allowed because of his "humble attitude" (!) when applying for the dispensation. It then took place on June 13, 1708 (probably an error as to the year unless it had been deffered for full twelve months).

Luis and Leonor might have had some children, at least a first one from those previous contacts, but there is no record about any such, due to those missing folios in the baptismal book mentioned previously. (Once I mentioned a female child named Antonia, but now cannot place the source for it.) Besides, the marriage was quite brief, for nine years later Leonor as a widow married again. According to her petition, Luis lay buried inside the Albuquerque church, but no date was given for his demise. And for whatever reasons she had, Leonor now chose a man who was not only twice her age, but one of those low-class *mestizo-mulato* individuals who had been born in Santa Fe's Analco prior to 1680.

Perhaps as a little girl, before her widowed mother had brought her and her two elder Montaño sisters down to Atrisco, she had fallen in love, as some little girls do, with the married adult's male charms. Then, upon reaching puberty in Atrisco, she had turned on her own charms upon the young son of Don Fernando in whose estate her mother and sisters lived, giving herself to him as a ruse so he would marry her. Her sister Magdalena later on might have done the same to lasso his brother Antonio, for, as we shall see later, her other sister Juana worked an identical trick to capture a third Chaves brother named Nicolás.

Young Leonor's second choice after Luis Chaves died was a Francisco de la Cruz de la Cadena, fifty years old, a native of New Mexico and resident of Santa Fe, the son of Francisco de la Cruz and Antonia de Ynojos. The father's "de la Cruz" surname happened to be a very common one among the mixed-breeds of Analco and elsewhere, originally derived from such baptismal names given them as Juan de la Cruz, María de la Cruz, and so forth. The mother's Ynojos surname easily suggests its origin from some Ynojos stud of the preceding century and a mixed-breed female servant. And all this is corroborated by the fact that Leonor's new groom had been widowed only two months before of Ana de la Cruz, a Tesuque Indian woman who had lived with him in Santa Fe and was buried there. The new marriage took place on November 1, 1716, very likely in Santa Fe, following which Leonor sold her former husband's portion of the Atrisco Chaves property to his elder brother Antonio.

All this shows that Luis Durán y Chaves had resided in Atrisco since 1705 with his parents and most of his brothers. Very likely old Don Fernando had felt more grief, not only because his son Luis had married one of the Montaño girls, but especially when he died so young, as had his eldest boy Bernardo some years before. Mercifully, he was spared the shame of Leonor's second marriage, when he would have said to the rest of the family, "I told you so."

2. *Criados and Genízaros*

The subsequent marriage of Luis Chaves' widow, and also the brevity of this particular section, provides a much needed break here for a thorough explanation of certain ethnic terms used heretofore, one which was promised in the very beginning. In the preceding century were those of *mestizo* and *mulato*. The first one, meaning "mixed," plainly denoted an admixture of Spanish and Indian. This in southern New Spain had a number of subtle gradations with their proper terminology. The very first step, *coyote*, designated anyone who was half-Spanish and half-Indian, from the belief that the animal of this name (Aztec *coyotl*) was part wolf and part dog. (Also used in New Mexico from the beginning, *coyote* finally came to mean the spawn of a native Hispanic and any outsider, whether European of any kind of "Anglo-American.") The last step in the *mestizo* gradaation was *castizo* (from *casta* or caste), after which one became a restored *español* under the right conditions. In New Mexico this term appears only in documents designating some of the Zacatecas colonists of 1695. (In Spain, however, *castizo* had always meant the "chasteness" or clear simplicity of the Castilían spirit and language.)

Then there was the term *mulato*, derived from *mula*, the mixed offspring of a jackass and a mare, and denoting the admixture of Spanish white and African black—and no less insulting than *coyote* as the mixture of wolf and dog. This, too, had its several gradations in African terms, but in New Mexico *mulato* was the only one used since earliest times for anyone said to have African origins no matter how remote. This referred to those individuals of lower caste who in the 1600s occasionally arrived with the Mission supply trains and decided to stay in Santa Fe's Analco, finally replacing its original Tlascaltec settlers. Except for this or that one who had gone to live at some Indian pueblo, the *mulatos* as well as the *mestizos* of Analco, and those who were servants at the various *estancias*, fled with the Spanish folk to El Paso del Norte when the Pueblo Revolt broke out in 1680. Practically all of them stayed down there when Governor Vargas brought back the colonists in 1693; descendants of anyone who did return, as well as some similar individuals from among the Zacatecas new colonists of 1695, and who kept intermarrying among themselves, were still being called either *mestizos* or *mulatos*, depending on each individual's skin shade or physiognomy. But still they were a minority.

Following the Vargas Reconquest, however, an entirely new type of admixture gradually arose under the name of *genízaros*. These were the offspring of what were called *criados*, Indians again but totally different from the previous ones of New Spain or Mexico. It was an eighteenth century ethnic phenomenon peculiar to New Mexico, and all this came about after 1700 from the practice of the better-endowed *españoles* of redeeming (*rescatando*) Plains Indian women and children whom the Comanches themselves had captured from other such tribes, these purchases being done during periods of truce. The tribes most often mentioned were *Pãnanas* (Pawnees), *Cãiguas* (Kiowas), and *Aãs* (Aish or Wichitas). Such purchases or "redemptions" were done with the earnest purpose of rearing the captives in the Christian Faith, endowing them with their masters' surnames and way of speech; at the same time there was the worldy advantage of acquiring free domestic help as well as herders for the flocks. Later on there would be others, such as Utes and Navajos, whom the Spanish themselves had taken in retaliatory forays against the so-called barbarians, just as the latter had captured

Spanish children.

They were all called *criados* in the two meanings of the Spanish word, first as "reared" in someone's home, and secondly as "servants." But they were not, as many outsiders have written, actually slaves. First of all, they were reared as part of the household; secondly, they were on their own when they reached adulthood and got married. And when they married each other, it was actually with *criados* and *criadas* of different Plains tribes, so that their mixed christianized and hispanized children no longer had a tribal identity. They were a new breed, as it were, and so the Spanish folk called them *genízaros*. This term had different ethnic meanings down in New Spain, a faulty derivation from a Turkish word for young prisoners trained to be bodyguards—and whence also the English word, janissary, came to denote auxiliary troops. But, as just said, for the New Mexicans it meant a new breed in the Indian world. Those in Santa Fe replaced the former *mestizos* and *mulatos* of Analco, and by century's end were settled on the Pecos river at San Miguel del Vado when this place was established there as a military post on the Comanche frontier, as well as at San José del Vado close by. For those living north of Santa Fe, the village of Abiquiú was founded early in the century, while those of the Río Abajo were first settled near Tomé and then were transferred to Los Jarales near Belén.

The term *genízaro* was dropped from common use a long time ago, but I myself remember some Hispanic parent calling a dark-complexioned child of his a *genízaro* or *genízara* as a term of endearment. And in more recent times, now that people are researching their ancestry, some who realize that they have Amerindian features or other characteristics—or have even researched their past—are proudly referring to themselves as *genízaros*. Others from different parts of our country, and of various nationalities, are also boasting about some Native American infusion in bygone days.

* * *

Coming back to our Chaves historical theme, we have seen, and shall see, how some of them had *criados*, and then *genízaros* and *coyotes* in their households, while also bearing the Chaves surname. As early as 1722 there is an Aparicio Chaves, nineteen and a native of New Mexico, the natural son of an *india Pânana* (Pawnee) of the Atrisco *estancia*, asking to marry a María Antonia de la Rosa, also known as La Prieta (the Dusky One). She is from among the Zacatecas *mestizos* living in Santa Fe's Analco. But the wedding did not take place until the following year when Aparicio was completely on his own and now a soldier at the Santa Fe garrison. Here the bride's name was given as María Rosa Velásquez, but referred to elsewhere as La Prieta.

Other such cases, but in which the former masters were not identified, are the following: In 1760, a Gregorio Chaves, twenty-two and a *coyote* of Atrisco, married a Jacinto Lucero in the Tomé parish, she being the widow of a Tomás González and daughter of Antonio Bonifacio Lucero and Barbara Sedillo, *coyotes*. Also in 1760, at Isleta, Mariano Chaves, a twenty-one-year-old, married María Pascuala Rivas, *coyota* of Tomé; and in 1768 this same *coyota* María Pascuala (now called Silva), and the widow of Mariano Chaves, married Felipe de Neri Baca, also a *coyote*. At Belén there was a couple named Francisco Silva and Petrona Chaves whose two sons, Simón and Santiago, were designated either as *indios* or *genízaros* between 1772 and 1780, and which also shows that the parents were of different Plains tribes. Likewise, in 1762 a María Antonio Chaves an *india* of Belén, had married a Lorenzo Francisco, this one a native *indio* of Ysleta del Paso, hence a descendant of the Isleta Pueblo Tiguas whom Governor Otermín had taken down there in 1681.

Many other such instances appear, some in the pre-nuptial documents and others in the marriage registers, or else in civil papers, which illustrate how the original Plains Indian *criados* and their mixed *genízaro* children, after having received their surnames from their previous owners, passed them on to posterity. With regard to some of the *coyotes* (half-breeds) named Chaves, or with any other outstanding surname, it suspiciously looks as though the original lords upstairs had been playing with the maids downstairs. So what? Even President Jefferson did it, and perhaps some others who signed our precious and glorious Declaration of Independence.

(And this reminds me of something unrelated to our theme, but prompted by this last, and rather disrespectful, remark. During our beloved Country's Bicentennial in 1976, I first came to notice that one of the Declaration's signers was a Chaves! There among those signatures of every description, and in neat small script, was the name of "*Samuel Chaves*." My Anglo-surnamed compatriots to whom I showed it smiled in puzzled disbelief but with no comment, until I pointed out that it was actually the signature of *Samuel Chase* of Maryland. The little squiggle at the end of it looked like an "s," and this in reverse suggestion made the middle "s" look like a "v." And privately, as a proud American, I keep cherishing this coincidence, no matter how far-fetched it actually is.)

VI. Nicolás Durán y Chaves

Juana Montaño

1. *Another Fruitful Brother*

In 1719 Nicolás acted as a pre-nuptial witness giving his age as twenty-six, hence born at El Paso del Norte around the year 1686. He was the sixth son of Don Fernando, and also residing with the family in Atrisco when he took the third one of the Montaño sisters to wife. Her name was *Juana Montaño*. This took place on July 20, 1714, when they already had at least one boy who was four years old. It had taken her that much more time to get her Chaves man. It could also have been a turbulent union for a time, since once, after he gave her a beating, she tried walking all the way to her own folks in Santa Fe before Nicolás caught up with her at Bernalillo. Yet they managed to produce a very large family of which we have a complete list, thanks to the extant will which he drew up on May 19, 1768. In it he stated the names of his parents, his wife, and the following eight sons and four daughters according to their ages: José, Gertrudis, Bernardo, Luis, Fernando, Isabel, Antonio, María Francisca, María Antonia, Juan, Vicente, María, and Francisco.

Of the four girls, there is further record only of the first three named in the will. The eldest one, as *Doña Gertrudis Durán y Chaves*, and fifteen in 1729, the daughter of Don Nicolás Chaves and Doña Juana Montaño, natives of New Mexico living in Atrisco, married Francisco Silva, thirty, a New Mexico native and the son of Antonio de Silva and Gregoria Ruíz, both natives of Mexico City.[1] This latter couple had come with the Mexico Valley colonists of 1694. The next daughter, *Isabel Chaves*, as we learn from the 1798 pre-nuptial investigation of a grandson, José Lugardo Padilla, had married a certain Padilla, and was there identified as a daughter of Nicolás Chaves, the brother of Antonio Chaves. The third one, *María Antonia Chaves* had three husbands, the first two having an interesting historical background.

On March 20, 1751, this María Antonia married Tadeo Romero, the son of Matías Romero and Angela Teresa Vallejo. He was descended in a direct line from Bartolomé Romero and Luisa Robledo, a married couple from Toledo which had

1. GENEALOGY: **Gertrudis D. y Chaves**, Agustina Silva, Lugarda Tafoya, Pablo Baca, Tomás Baca, Nicanora Baca, Fabián Chávez, Fr. A. Chávez.

arrived in 1598; Bartolomé was Oñate's artillery captain who made the conquest of Ácoma possible in that year, and both were the parents of that Doña Ana Robledo, wife of Francisco Gómez, who in 1622 had invited Governor Sotelo and Doña Isabel de Bohórques, wife of Don Pedro de Chaves, to act as godparents for their first child, Francisco Gómez Robledo. On the other hand, Angela Teresa Vallejo had come from Mexico City in 1694 as a little orphan girl with her Vallejo father, her mother having died during the long journey; she had first married a Miguel Lucero by whom she had some children, and then Matías Romero by whom she had this Tadeo Romero.[2]

Finally, in 1768, Doña María Antonia Chaves, forty and the widow of Tadeo Romero, daughter of Don Nicolás de Chaves and Doña Juana Montaño, married a Domingo Baca, thirty, an *español* of San Gabriel de las Nutrias whose parents were not given. A witness was her youngest brother Francisco who lived in El Rancho de Guadalupe (Los Chaves) in the Isleta district.

Now to what we know about the eight sons of Nicolás Durán y Chaves and Juana Montaño.

2. *Odd Notes in the Octet*

1. *José Chavez* married María Luisa Aragón on February 3, 1732, and seems to have been a normal fellow plagued by certain troubles, although we know of only one interesting episode in connection with his good wife and a grandchild of theirs. In 1766 his widow brought suit against a Don Pedro Yturrieta for trying to impede the wedding of her grand-daughter María Rita Yturrieta, whom she had reared since infancy. This fellow, the son of a newcomer to New Mexico and of unknown origin, had married her daughter María Chaves on May 17, 1751; subsequently, and much against his wife's will, he had gone off to Mexico City and stayed there for more than a year. Meanwhile María Chaves had given birth to their child, this María Rita, but whom he refused to acknowledge as his upon his return. Ever since then Luisa Aragón and her late husband had brought up this their grandchild, and now, after all these years, her estranged father was trying to interfere with her wedding.

All of the witnesses who were called to testify strongly spoke in Luisa's favor,

2. GENEALOGY: **María Antonia D. y Chaves**, Manuela Romero, José Encarnación Chaves, José Francisco Chaves, Eugenio Chávez, Fabián Chávez, Fr. A. Chávez.

and she appears to have won the case. Yet, Pedro Yturrieta and his wife María Chaves must have gotten together again following his return from Mexico City and his refusal to acknowledge the first girl as his own child. Whether he accepted her or not after a period of time, her Aragón grandmother had insisted on keeping her as her own ward. All this one gathers from the fact that the couple had another child who, at Belén in 1776, as Petra Vitalia Yturrieta, *española* and the daughter of Pedro Yturrieta and María Chaves, married a Bartolomé Trujillo.

---

2. *Bernardo Chaves* was the real oddball among his brothers. He was already forty-two and still unmarried in 1762 when, as Don Bernardo Durán y Chaves, *español* of San Clemente, the son of the *capitán* Don Nicolás Durán y Chaves and Doña Juana Montño, also of San Clemente (Los Lunas), asked to marry none other than a woman named simply María de la Luz. She was an *india criada* of the Aá Nation, and old Don Fernando would have spun in his grave, were this possible for mere dust and ashes.

Now, ethnologists whom I have consulted have been unable to identify this Aá tribe, often mentioned in the records. But this is most likely the solution. Far back in 1542, Coronado's men had found a Plains Indian settlement called *Haxa* (pronounced "Asha"), and the early Franciscan chroniclers of New Spain then wrote that Fray Juan de Padilla, the first North American martyr, had been killed in that year by wild Indians called *haciaëles* or *aciales*. Decades ago, the eminent Dr. F. W. Hodge identified all such old terms with a Wichita tribe called the Aiish, hence oldish Bernardo's bride could well have been a Wichita.

There is no record of any children Bernardo and his squaw might have had during their brief marriage, for she was dead by 1771 when the aging widower tried to marry again. In this very year, at Isleta, Don Bernardo Durán y Chaves, *español* and forty-four, and of El Puesto de Guadalupe (Los Chaves), the son of Don Nicolás Durán y Chaves, deceased, and Doña Juana Montaño, and widowed of María Luz *Benavides* (surname of her original master), asked to marry María Josefa Núñez, *española* and forty, the widow of Cristóbal Chaves and a native of Mexico City residing at El Puesto de San Andrés. Here is where the oldish squawman Bernardo claimed that there was no need for a dispensation for him to marry his first cousin's widow, saying that Cristóbal Chaves was not the son of Antonio Chaves but an adulterous son of his wife Antonia Baca by an Eusebio Rael de Aguilar (that young swain of 1718 who had tried to marry Don Fernando's eldest daughter Isabel!). Anyway, the marriage did not take place because of the outlandish charges he had brought up.

---

3. *Luis Chaves* married a Bárbara Yturrieta on April 20, 1742. We know that he was a son of Nicolás from an 1838 pre-nuptial investigation in which he was designated as a brother of Vicente Chaves (son of Nicolás), and the father of an Isabel Chaves who was a first cousin of Vicente's son Francisco Chaves.

---

4. *Fernando Chaves*, the fourth son of Nicolás, was not the man of this name who married an Antonia Sánchez as I had previously supposed, he being most likely the eldest son of Antonio Chaves and his short-lived first wife. This Fernando, who married a María Quintana, was the one, and we know it from a daughter of theirs, Doña María Cayetana Durán y Chaves, nineteen and of the Isleta district, the daughter of Don Fernando Durán y Chaves and Doña María Quintana, deceased, who in June 1769 married a third cousin of hers named Andrés Torres of Sabinal, the son of José Torres and María Francisca Silva; here the bride's father was identified as the son of Don Nicolás Durán y Chaves, the latter being the son of Lucía Hurtado.

Other known children of this Fernando were: *Ángel Francisco Chaves*, *español* and twenty-five, the son of "Bernardo" Chaves and María Quintana, deceased, who in 1773 at Belén married Feliciana Gallegos, twenty-three, the daughter of Manuel Gallegos and Gertrudis Silva; *Susana Chaves*, *española* and seventeen, daughter of "Bernardo" Chaves and María Quintana, deceased, who in 1774 at Belén married José María González, *español* and twenty, the son of José González and Teodora Gutiérrez; *Manuel Chaves*, *español* and thirty, son of "Bernardo" Chaves and María Quintana, deceased, who in 1775 at Belén married Josefa Baca of unknown parentage; and, finally, *Toribio Durán y Chaves*, *español* of Alameda and thirty-five, the son of "Bernardo" Chaves and María Quintana, both of them deceased, and he himself widowed of Andréa Quiteria García de Noriega; in June of 1781 he married Gertrudis González, *española* of Los Ranchos de Albuquerque, she being the daughter of Cristóbal González and Rita Jurado.

Here we have a case of a first name like *Hernando* or *Fernando* becoming intermixed with *Bernardo*, as were the female names *Luisa* and *Lucía*, to the future confusion of anyone doing family research. In this particular case, the investigation for the marriage of the first daughter, along with a family tree, definitely show that the father's name was Fernando, and the son of Nicolás. Besides, we have seen that his elder brother, Bernardo, was a distinctly different person both as to his character and marital adventures. And from a Gabaldón family tree of 1838, this same Fernando, the son of Nicolás, had another daughter named Victoria Chaves who had married a Trujillo and had a daughter named Isabel.

A similar but not quite the same variation occurred in 1773 when a Rosa Chaves, forty, of San Clemente, *criada* in the house of Don Hernando (Fernando) Chaves, married a Juan Cristóbal Silva, *coyote* of Fuenclara. Then another such occurred in 1780 when a Juan Manuel Chaves, *coyote* and twenty-four, the natural son of that same Rosa Chaves who was a *criada* of Hernando Chaves, married a Rosa Serna, *española*.

---

5. *Antonio Chaves*, the next son of Nicolás. From a careful investigation of others having the same name, he was in all probability this son who listed in his father's will. At Isleta on April 13, 1750, he married Barbara Padilla, the daughter of Diego de Padilla and María Vásquez Baca. Two of their children whom we know from their own respective marriages were María Gertrudis and Santiago, and both of them are here singled out and treated at some length because of particular descendants each of them had.

At Los Chaves on February 12, 1775, *Gertrudis Chaves*, *española* and twenty-five, the daughter of Antonio Chaves and Barbara Padilla, married Miguel Gabaldón of San Clemente, *español* and forty, the son of Don Juan Gabaldón and Doña Juliana Archibeque. (In the marriage record the groom's name is Miguel Baltasar.) This groom's Gabaldón father, whose full name was Juan Manuel, was a native of Puebla who had come to live at first with his uncle or elder brother, the Franciscan Fray Antonio Gabaldón (the padre who performed his marriage with the Archibeque woman on July 26, 1735, and who also was the executor of his last will). As for Juan Manuel's bride, she was the grand-daughter of Jean l'Archevêque, a Frenchman from Bayonne who had played a minor part in the ambush murder of his master, Robert de La Salle, after the latter's naval expedition foundered on the Texas Gulf coast back in 1684; then he had come to New Mexico with the Vargas forces of 1693.

Gertrudis Chaves and Miguel Gabaldón had at least five sons and five daughters. One girl, Juana María Gabaldón, came to marry José Enrique Luna in 1796. This Luna's maternal line, as shown elsewhere, came down from a Chaves great-grandmother (Josefa Chaves, Pedro Chaves' daughter and wife of Francisco Sánchez), and his Gabaldón wife who had a Chaves mother; they produced several children who for the first time after two hundred years of New Mexico history made the Luna name one of the most prominent ones of the past and present centuries. One of the sons did not, for his having died young along with his wife. He was Toribio Luna, born on April 16, 1799, who had married a María Manuela Montaño, both of them leaving behind two little orphans named María Encarnación and José Dolores Luna. The girl, when only twelve, married José Francisco Chaves in Belén on October 3, 1845, and both joined other members of his landless family in seeking a new home as pioneers in what is now Mora County.[3] Her little brother who went along eventually married a Guadalupe Baca at San Miguel del Vado in 1851.

But a younger living son of José Enrique Luna and Juana María Gabaldón, and who had inherited plenty of land and livestock in what is now Los Lunas, was *Antonio José Luna, born in 1808, who married an Isabel Baca. Among their children were Tranquilino, Salomón, and Eloisa Luna, all of whom came to form the nucleus of high society in the last century, both in politics and commerce. Tranquilino Luna, besides serving as a Deputy in Congress, 1880-1882, outdid himself in the military, whence old Camp Luna near Las Vegas got the name.*

Here, as in the case of the Cabeza de Bacas and others, is another small dynasty which had gotten its start with a Chaves woman in both the paternal and maternal lines, hence also with now remote connections with Cíbola and Analco.

Another daughter of Gertrudis Chaves and Miguel Gabaldón was Ana María Gabaldón who married José Ignacio Gallegos of Abiquiú, and who became the mother of *Padre José Manuel Gallegos of Albuquerque. As a young priest he was ousted from his parish, and also suspended on false charges, by Bishop Lamy of Santa Fe in 1852. He then ran for Congress and became the first duly-elected*

3. GENEALOGY: **Gertrudis Chaves**, Juana María Gabaldón, Toribio Luna, María Encarnación Luna, Eugenio Chávez, Fabián Chávez, Fr. A. Chávez.

Representative of New Mexico in our country's Capital.—His mendacious arch-foe, Vicar Machebeuf, described him in French as "very spirited and handsome," and therefore as a vain womanizer which he falsely concluded. Hence the partly French title, *Très Macho—He Said*, for my biography of Padre Gallegos.

A brother of Gertrudis, *Santiago Chaves*, *español* of the Isleta district, as the son of Antonio Chaves and Barbara Padilla, married Margarita Varela, *española* of Tomé, the daughter of Juan Varela and Feliciana Montoya, in March of 1775. His writing skills were soon being employed by the padres in drawing up matrimonial investigations, several samples of which survive from the years 1783 and 1789, and in which he signed his full name as Santiago Durán y Chaves. Four years after the marriage Margarita was dead, as also Santiago's parents, when in August of 1781 Santiago married a third cousin, María Luz García, *española*, daughter of Toribio García and Antonia Teresa Gutiérrez. These had a son, Don Ramón Chaves of Valencia, who on April 7, 1823 married Dolores Sánchez, the daughter of a younger Don Jacinto Sánchez and his wife Doña Gertrudis Castillo. Then these had a son on February 4, 1825, whom they named *Manuel Felipe de Jesús, and who came to be ordained a priest by Bishop Lamy. This alone, however, is not what made Padre Manuel Felipe Chaves stand out in local annals. When quite young he had first married in Tomé a Luján girl who died young, leaving him with a two-year-old child named Demetrio; then the good French pastor of Tomé, Father Jean-Baptiste Rallière, who was an unassuming scholar, trained him in theology and related subjects for his ordination on Sept. 24, 1859.*

Right after this, Padre Chaves began doing pioneer work for his bishop. He was the first priest whom Lamy sent to faraway Tucson in southernmost Arizona when that area became part of his diocese, and from there he sent him east to the new town of Las Cruces to do the same pioneer work there. Years later, while pastor of San Ysidro near Jémez, and feeling his end approaching, he went down to his brother's house in Valencia where he died in 1881. There his funeral was by far the largest ever seen in those parts, attended also by many of the French Río Abajo clergy and the Italian Jesuits of Albuquerque, who later published a glowing obituary in their *Revista Católica* in Las Vegas. But of homelier interest is the career of his legitimate son Demetrio, whose education his father had seen to; he grew up to be a fine gentleman, ending up at Las Cruces where Padre Chaves had served. There he got married and became the ancestor of prominent Chaves and other families, some with Anglo surnames, in that southernmost part of modern New Mexico which had been acquired from Mexico through the Gadsden Purchase.

Incidentally, there was a previous young Chaves priest when Bishop Lamy and his aide Machebeuf arrived in 1851, *Rafael Chaves* by name, but whose family origin is obscure. He was a rather silly fellow, but the bishop treated him with forebearance while his vicar went after him with tooth and nail. Most likely he was born in the Cebolleta country, for, when the good Rio Grande parishes were being given to the new French clergy, he left the ministry and went to live in Cebolleta where he got married.

---

6. *Juan Chaves* was referred to on April 16, 1761, as Don Juan Durán y Chaves of the Isleta district, *español* and twenty-eight, and the son of Don Nicolás Durán y Chaves and Doña Juana Montaño, when he married Doña Magdalena Varela of Alameda, *española* and eighteen, the daughter of Don Pedro Varela and Doña Casilda González, deceased. So far it is not known if they had any children.

---

7. *Vicente Chaves*, also listed in his father's will, can be further identified as a son of Nicolas D. y Chaves through some family connections. As a brother of Luis and Fernando Chaves previously treated, he was married to a Gertrudis Sánchez. They had a daughter named Victoria Chaves who in 1774, as an *española* and twenty, the daughter of Vicente Chaves and Gertrudis Sánchez, was asked for in marriage by Vicente Luna, also an *español* and twenty, the son of Domingo Luna and Josefa Lucero, both deceased.

But here a puzzle is posed by a certain matrimonial investigation of that same year of 1774. Vicente Luna had first asked to marry a María Barbara Chaves, daughter of Francisco D. y Chaves; but she was a first and second cousin, and for some reason the wedding did not take place. It was then that Vicente Luna asked to marry that Victoria Chaves, daughter of Vicente Chaves, and here a matrimonial witness testified that the pair were not first cousins as in the previous case because her father Vicente Chaves was not really a son of Nicolás, brother of Francisco D. y Chaves! Whether this allegation was true or not, the marriage of Luna and Victoria seems to have taken place, with or without the required dispensations. As for Victoria Chaves herself, she later contracted marriage during October of 1782 with Juan Francisco Pino of Los Lunas, the son of Don Mateo José Pino and Doña Teresa Sánchez, both deceased (and also treated previously in connections with Pedro Bautista Pino). Here they were dispensed from a large number of relationships, from straight second cousins to second and third oblique cousins by blood, and from first and third cousins by affinity.

There was also a son, Francisco Chaves, identified as a son of Vicente Chaves and a nephew of Luis Chaves in a pre-nuptial investigation of 1838. This was when María Serafina Chaves, daughter of this younger Don Francisco Chaves, deceased, and Doña María Antonia Montoya, in 1838 married a José Torres, son of Don José María Torres and Doña Juana Baca, the pair being related twice in various degrees as descendants of both Luis and Vicente Chaves.

---

8. *Francisco Chaves*, the youngest son of Nicolás Durán y Chaves, married María Gertrudis Álvarez del Castillo, born February 12, 1743, a daughter of Juan Miguel Álvarez del Castillo, mentioned previously as being of unknown origin, and his first wife Barbara Baca, sister of the *capitán* Baltasar Baca. Three known children of this Francisco Chaves were the following:

1) Doña Maria Barbara Durán y Chaves, *española* of San Clemente, the daughter of Don Francisco Durán y Chaves and Doña Gertrudis Álvarez del Castillo, who in 1775 married a José Francisco Pino, *español* and twenty-five, but of parents unknown; five years later she was dead when Pino remarried in 1780, naming a Barbara Sánchez as his natural mother.
2) María de la Luz Chaves, sixteen, of El Rancho de Guadalupe (in Los Chaves), daughter of Francisco Chaves and María Gertrudis Álvarez del Castillo, deceased, married Felipe de Jesús Varela in 1780; an *español* and twenty-six, he was the son of Pedro Varela and Casilda González, deceased. 3) Baltasar de los Reyes Durán y Chaves, *español* of Los Chaves, the son of Francisco Durán y Chaves and María Álvarez del Castillo, deceased, in 1783 married María Gertrudis Romero of the same place, the daughter of Andrés Romero and Antonia Jaramillo, after they were duly dispensed as second and third cousins on both their parents' sides.

* * *

Of such a wide variety of sons and daughters was the big family of Nicolás Durán y Chaves composed. It had started out at Atrisco, but later we find the parents already residing in the Isleta district, where Nicolás acquired considerable property and was involved in several land exchanges and litigations. As early as 1743 he had bought some land from that Bernabé Baca who had married the Mata daughter of his sister Isabel.—He also had his Indian *criados*. In December 1760, Juan Chaves, twenty-two, *criado* of Don Nicolás de Chaves in the Isleta district, married a Rosa Anaya, twenty, of Fuenclara. Also in this same month and year, another Juan Chaves, twenty-one (if not the same person), *coyote* and *criado* of Don Nicolás de Chaves, married a María Paula Rivas, a *coyota* of Tomé. In 1762, Juan Francisco Chaves Ribera, twenty-three, a *coyote* and *criado* of the *capitán* Nicolás Duran y Chaves, married a Josefa Gallegos, eighteen and a *mestiza*, who was also a *criada* of the same Nicolás. One of the witnesses was Don Bernardo Durán y Chaves, forty-two (that son of Nicolás who had married a Wichita squaw).

Like his elder brothers Pedro and Antonio, and Francisco to some extent, Nicolás had produced a very large family, most members of which did the same. Whatever the background of their marriage partners, old Don Fernando would have been proud to see such a grand proliferation of his genes and the Chaves name. His eldest son Bernardo, on whom he had placed his hope, had not been near as lucky, nor that other son named Luis; and another such example would be the youngest of his seven sons, Pedro Gómez, whom he had named after his own grandfather, the Extremaduran noble founder of the clan when the Kingdom of New Mexico, a "miserable" one in certain respects, was brand-new.

VII. Pedro Gómez Durán y Chaves

Petrona Martín Serrano

His Father's Last Hope

This was the tenth and last child in the family of Don Fernando Durán y Chaves, born at El Paso del Norte sometime prior to the Reconquest by Don Diego de Vargas in 1693, and whom his father, homesick for his New Mexico while dwelling on what he deemed a noble family past, decided to christen with the full name of his own grandfather, Don Pedro Gómez Durán of 1600. Even if it was a "miserable kingdom" to which he yearned to return at a time when all of his Chaves relations were abandoning their home by moving down to New Spain, his thoughts had been dwelling more and more on the great deeds performed by that pioneer grandfather—and then by his eldest son, the first Don Fernando, whose name he now proudly bore.

Then, following his return around 1696 to his ancestral *estancia* of El Tunque, which since his father Fernando's day was already reduced to a smaller Bernalillo homestead he had named after his little Bernardo, he had experienced the tragic death of this his favorite firstborn in 1705, after which he got rid of the property with its sad memories and followed his other sons to the estates they acquired in Atrisco. And here his fixation about a "miserable kingdom" came most strongly to the fore, as already shown so dramatically, because of the radical changes fast occurring with the arrival of what he deemed less desirable new colonists, as well as the rise in influence of some of the older ones whom he had considered beneath his station. At least subconsciously, he was also disturbed by the type of marriages being entered into by his remaining sons.

And so Don Fernando might have pinned his hopes on this his youngest son Pedro Gómez to restore and revive some of the past glory of his Chaves inheritance, but he died when the young fellow must have been less than twenty years old. At this time Pedro Gómez was being referred to as *Pedro Chaves el Mozo* (the Younger) to distinguish him from his much older brother also named Pedro. He also had the nickname *Perico*, Old Spanish for "Little Pete," and perhaps used by his father since he was a baby, just as he had called his favorite firstborn *Bernalillo*, which is likewise Old Spanish for "Little Bernie." This youngest Pedro Gómez was still living with the family at Atrisco in 1732, the year he sold the lands of his inheritance to that Bernabé Baca mentioned before, and to Antonia Baca, the widow of his elder brother Antonio.

And why he did so poses a question, one which can be partly answered from a surprising entry in the marriage register of Santa Cruz de la Cañada north of Santa Fe.

There, on July 6, 1737, Pedro Gómez de Chaves married a Petrona Martín, no parents given either for the groom or for the bride, yet leaving no doubt that he was Don Fernando's youngest son. And Petrona herself had to be from among the very many Martín Serrano people who inhabited the northern mountain country. Moreover, Pedro Gómez was the very first Chaves in almost a century and a half of New Mexico history to choose any such northern bride and take up his residence in what was called the Río Arriba as opposed to the Río Abajo south of Santa Fe. And why he took such a drastic action makes one suspect that he had grown tired of the squabbles rampant in the Río Abajo among the fast-growing and closely intermarried families of his elder brothers, not to mention their numerous Baca and other in-laws. Or could it be that he remembered his father counselling him as a growing boy to be different, to do something different, from what his other sons had been doing thus far with no distinguishing accomplishments to be proud of? This is a mere supposition.

What he did was something different: he left his Atrisco heritage and relatives, something quite brave but, unfortunately rather foolhardy. For he did not choose to reside peaceably in the major town of Santa Cruz or its fertile ravine of Chimayó, nor among the several other settlements throughout the large Santa Clara valley. This can be understood, since part of the land belonged to the several Tewa pueblos from times beyond recall, while the rest belonged to Spanish families either from generations past or from grants made by Governor Vargas to some of his leading officers. Hence there was only one recourse: with some other northern individuals who also needed new territory for their livelihood, he decided to start his own family empire in a place called Ojo Caliente.

In those days this picturesque ravine with its now famous thermal springs lay most isolated and wholly unprotected within that very large triangle formed by the juncture of the Rio Chama and the Rio Grande. Bands of the enemy Utes and Jicarilla Apaches from the north were known to visit the area, very likely to avail themselves of the hot springs on occasion. Because of this no one had dared to live there heretofore until around the time when Pedro Gómez and Petrona Martín were married. And soon, besides the Spanish folk who had moved into the area, there were several Indians, some as *criados* and others as incipient family groups of free *genízaros*. The baptismal book of the Santa Clara Mission carries the baptisms in 1743 of six children from among several adult Plains Indians who in years past had been ransomed from the Comanches, as well as some other Apache captives.

Otherwise, the early history of Ojo Caliente is little known for lack of documentation. There are conflicting reports about the place having been abandoned for a time because of the enemy Indian menace from the north, and it is known for certain that the Utes and Apaches did wipe out the settlement, along with others in the Taos valley, sometime prior to 1776.

All that we have about our Pedro Gómez Durán y Chaves consists of a few scattered jottings in the Mission register of Santa Clara, whose current friar had Ojo Caliente as his mission territory at the time. On February 2, 1742, we find Pedro Gómez de Chaves and Petrona Martín, five years after their marriage, acting as godparents for Juana, an *india* of Ojo Caliente; whether a child or an adult, she was evidently one of those Plains Indians ransomed from the Comanches. In the following year, April 24, three Apache children were baptized, the three being *criados* belonging to a Juan Lobato and a Blas Martín. Here Pedro Gómez stood as godfather for little Gertrudis and María Antonia, while a young Antonia Chaves was the godmother of the third child who was named José. This Antonia was presumably Pedro's daughter, only eight or so at the time. The last such entry is on April 20, 1746, when again Pedro Gómez and Petrona Martín were the godparents of an Antonio Arias, *español* of Ojo Caliente, hence the child of an Arias couple living there.

This is the last notice we have so far about Pedro Gómez Durán y Chaves and his family. Nor do we know what other children he might have had, or if any descendants of his are some of the Chaves folk who appear in the early church and civil records of the north country. In 1760, a *Juan Bernardo* of Ojo Caliente, using the full name of *Durán y Chaves*, married a María de Loreto (no last name given), also of Ojo Caliente. He could well have been a son or grandson of Pedro Gómez, but there is no corroboration as yet. And did this Juan Bernardo with others of his brethren and relatives perish when the Utes or Apaches wiped out the settlement around this time?

Other northern Chaves folk are more likely descended from that Blas Durán y Chaves, son of Eusebio and grandson of Don Fernando's second son named Pedro, and who got the *alcaldía* of Abiquiú around the year 1775. Much later there was that Francisco Antonio Chaves with his wife Rosalía Velarde, married at Sandía in 1797, who subsequently moved north to that same place and became the parents of General José María Chaves of the Civil War, and of Julián Chaves of Los Angeles' Chávez Ravine. A very much later Chaves arrived in the Santa Cruz valley in 1843. He was a Manuel Chaves of Los Padillas and twenty-six, the son of Rafael Chaves and María Gertrudis Padilla, who came north to marry a María del Carmen Abeyta, fifteen, the daughter of Bernardo Abeyta and Manuela Trujillo of Chimayó. This explains the Chaves tombstones in front of the famous Santuario built by that Abeyta.

Conclusion

To sum up the entire Chávez saga as told here in fullest detail, old Don Fernando's dream about his youngest son Perico, if ever he did have such a dream, came to naught as it had done long before with the early death of the eldest one whom he had nicknamed Bernalillo. Four of the other sons in-between at least did their part genetically by fathering a vast clan bearing his name, not to mention those descended on the distaff side with different other surnames. Had Bernardo, Luis, and Pedro Gómez done the same, his New Mexico would now be enriched—or infested as the case may be—with twice the number of Chávez people she now has.

To this day there have been further outstanding descendants of good Don Fernando, whether bearing his name one way or another, but only their respective groups can tell us who they are. One could name several Chávez individuals, including some of one's own family as well as others with different surnames having a strong Chávez background, who in our own times have been prominent in government, in the various professions, and the military. But to name the ones who come to mind would rightfully incur the ire of many who likewise deserve mention. It devolves upon them to enter any such facts and data on blank pages of this book as a documented legacy for their own descendants.

Indeed, dear old Don Fernando up in the sky could derive adequate consolation from such latter descendants of his, whatever their surnames may be, and in a beloved homeland which, although not the royal kingdom that he knew, is no longer a miserable one as an integral part of the United States of America.

This great Country of ours was only seventy years old (1776-1846) when, thanks be to God, we became a part of the best Nation on earth and have served her faithfully ever since.

* * *

Had the late Duchess of Noblejas known the full story just told, she would not have called me her relative and given me that handsome crest. Yet, who knows? Witty Lady that she was, she might have chuckled many a time while perusing the varied fortunes of her own noble forebears going back eight centuries. There had to be first cousins marrying each other to consolidate inheritances or to keep the regal bloodline pure; here or there a violent death occurred for similar reasons or else out of a fit of jealousy.

More dramatically, a proud *Cristiano Viejo* ("Old Christian" supposedly untainted by Moorish or Jewish blood) acknowledged some child by a *morena* or a *marrana* of these two main classes, or even by a *gitana* from some gypsy camp. For all the way down the many past centuries, as we know from the history of the European royal and ducal families, princes and dukes liked to play around, even elevating a lady of the night to share their thrones with them, or having bastard sons to succeed them. Again, it is the old story of Adam mourning the fratricidal murder of his son Abel, of Judah consorting with Tamar at the crossroads, and of David weeping over his rebellious concubinic son Absalom.

Still, after all is said and done, family research like this one may have little value beyond the curiosity which prompted it, and yet certain historical events do come into better focus while certain blurry areas are clarified (such as the Pueblo Revolt of 1680). In a way, such research can also be termed quixotic—and, curiously enough, it was during the very years when New Mexico was first settled that Cervantes was composing his story of Don Quixote, and basing the fellow's wonderful madness on his pathetic belief of being descended from his imaginary noble house of Dulcinea del Toboso.

In our own times that masterful English author, Graham Greene, in his novel entitled *Monsignor Quixote*, carried the theme further with this funny but most poignant tale about a current Spanish country priest who believed that he was descended from Don Quixote's very own family, and then went about tilting at social and ecclesiastical windmills to the great discomfiture of his superiors. All this does suggest that both *Fray* Quixote and Monsignor Quixote have shared the same windmills with the original classic creation of Miguel de Cervantes.

CPSIA information can be obtained
at www.ICGtesting.com
Printed in the USA
BVHW092348100720
583349BV00003B/170